MW01286236

Advance Praise for *Broadway General Manager*

"An absolutely indispensable theater lover's guide to how Broadway works."

—Peter Marks, Chief Theater Critic, Washington Post

"*Broadway General Manager* is a must-read for any new producer entering the world of Broadway. And it is a wonderful tool for the novice general manager to hone their craft of being a general manager—one of the least understood yet certainly one of the most important members of the producing team. Peter's book takes the reader through the extraordinary number of details required to be a general manager and will help the potential new producer select just the right GM for their show. Every producer has a different set of skills, and the best producing teams ensure that the GM complements the producer's strengths. From budgets to contracts, there are excellent examples that will help the reader understand the myriad of things a producer needs from a GM."

—Charlotte St. Martin, President, the Broadway League

"Peter Bogyo's book is an invaluable guide to the work of a general manager and the way a GM fits into the process of making a commercial show. His love of his subject and of the theater shines through unmistakably in every chapter."

—Tom Viertel, six-time Tony Award®–winning producer and Executive Director of the Commercial Theater Institute

"*Broadway General Manager* is a valuable guide to the functions of a theatrical general manager, including clear and detailed explanations of production budgets, contracts, and other critical documents. Because general management touches on all aspects of commercial theater production, the book will be useful to anyone—artist or manager—interested in understanding the production process. Peter Bogyo's insightful commentary reflects his deep experience and demonstrates that ethicality, a sense of humor, and love for the art of theater are essential qualities for a successful general manager."

—Joan Channick, Chair of Theater Management, Yale School of Drama

"An essential work for theatre management, producing, and arts administration students. From budgets to contracts and beyond, *Broadway General Manager* makes a case for the crucial role of the general manager, addressing complex business issues, along with the idiosyncrasies of the theatre industry, and breaking them down in an engaging and easy-to-understand manner. Although the focus is commercial Broadway production, most of the book would be extremely useful for future not-for-profit managers as well. It is a welcome addition to our curriculum."

—Steven Chaikelson, Director,
MFA Theatre Management & Producing Program,
Columbia University School of the Arts

To Miriam —

BROADWAY
GENERAL
MANAGER

DEMYSTIFYING
THE MOST IMPORTANT
AND LEAST UNDERSTOOD ROLE
IN SHOW BUSINESS

So pleased to meet you!

Peter Bogyo

PETER BOGYO

Allworth Press

Allworth Press books may be purchased in bulk at special discounts for sales promotion, corporate gifts, fund-raising, or educational purposes. Special editions can also be created to specifications. For details, contact the Special Sales Department, Allworth Press, 307 West 36th Street, 11th Floor, New York, NY 10018 or info@skyhorsepublishing.com.

21 20 19 18 17   5 4 3 2 1

Published by Allworth Press, an imprint of Skyhorse Publishing, Inc. 307 West 36th Street, 11th Floor, New York, NY 10018. Allworth Press® is a registered trademark of Skyhorse Publishing, Inc.®, a Delaware corporation.

www.allworth.com

Cover design by Frank Fraver Verlizzo

Library of Congress Cataloging-in-Publication Data is available on file.

Print ISBN: 978-1-62153-624-6
Ebook ISBN: 978-1-62153-625-3

Printed in the United States of America

CONTENTS

ACKNOWLEDGMENTS

Special thanks to the following friends and colleagues for their invaluable input (in chronological order of its receipt!): Peter Shoemaker, Laura Heller, Nancy di Benedetto, Robert Lindsey-Nassif, David Friedlander, and Mitch Weiss.

Also, to all the producers, general managers, and company managers I have worked for, learned from, and been mentored by, especially Albert Poland, Roger Gindi, Ben Sprecher, Nelle Nugent, Marion Finkler Taylor, and Nancy Nagel Gibbs—I wouldn't be where I am today without the opportunities to learn and grow you provided for me. Thank you.

An extra special shout out to Tad Crawford of Allworth Press for his early belief in this book and for his invaluable input in developing it. Not to mention his actually publishing it.

I am deeply indebted to Frank "FRAVER" Verlizzo for the stunning front cover design he contributed to this book. It's not so easy to make a book about general managers look exciting and glamorous.

Finally, to my wife, Ahna McCracken Bogyo, my profoundest gratitude for your continual love, support, pride, and encouragement. With all the vagaries of show business, you remind me what is really important in life.

INTRODUCTION

I first fell in love with theater when I was five.

That year I was cast as the lead in my kindergarten's (nondancing!) production of *The Nutcracker*. In hindsight, my casting had much to do with being the tallest in the class. Nonetheless, I was hooked for life.

After graduating from Yale College in 1977, I came to New York to be an actor and studied with Stella Adler and William Esper. Seven years later, I discovered an original script with a fascinating role I was determined to play. After considerable mulling, I realized the best way to ensure I got the role was to produce the play myself, as an Off–Off Broadway showcase. I succeeded in this goal, but to my surprise, when I compared producing to acting, I had to admit I was better at producing!

More mulling ensued. I realized the two things I knew a producer had to do—namely, choose the property and raise the money—weren't things anybody could teach me. However, as I talked to various people and did my research, I became aware that there was another, more mysterious role—that of a **general manager** (**GM**)—that entailed working closely with a producer and possessing a vast knowledge of how Broadway worked. But what exactly did a GM do?

I assumed he or she must "manage" something "generally," but what *was* it?

This book will attempt to answer that question. Armed now with the benefit of more than thirty years of professional experience in the commercial theater, seventeen of which have been as the GM of ten Broadway and seven Off-Broadway shows, I only wish I had had such a book when I started out.

What I discovered (after going to work for several GMs to unearth the mysteries of the job) was that general managers oversee all the financial and business concerns of a show. Even more, they are the linchpin of the entire production, upon which every aspect of the show must rely. This includes budgeting, contract negotiation, financial overview, helping to establish the new business entity that will produce the play, setting up the box office, overseeing the paying of bills and taxes, calculating royalties and profit distributions, making sure insurance is secured, supervising and reviewing the marketing and advertising campaigns, hiring all cast, staff, and crew (and firing them if there is "just cause"), distributing accounting statements and end-of-year tax forms to the investors, advising on the timing of closing the show, etc. Part of what makes the general manager's job so exciting is that he interacts with people at every level of the production—producers, lawyers, accountants, investors, theater owners, designers, actors, agents, press agents, advertising agencies, casting agents, box office treasurers—and is expected to be available to the show's producer twenty-four/seven.

This book will explore these areas in detail and includes in-depth analysis of actual Broadway budgets and contracts. In no way is this book intended to replace the services of a general manager. Rather, it is hoped the book will give a greater understanding of what a GM does and how important his role is. A GM not only has extensive knowledge of the rules of Broadway's various unions, guilds, and societies, but he also possesses a breadth of experience, intuition, financial acumen, discretion, a network of personal relationships that can be called upon in times of need, and, finally, to quote Rudyard Kipling, the ability "to keep your head when all about you are losing theirs." No book could ever replace such a person, and it would be folly to try.

Although I long ago shed my "Nutcracker" dreams of acting, I have found great satisfaction in the theater as a general manager. I hope this book will help you appreciate this "most important and least understood" role and, perhaps, inspire you.

1

How Does One Become a General Manager?

Just as all roads lead to Rome, there are multiple paths one can take to become a general manager. Some people go to graduate school for arts administration. Others intern, serve as an assistant, apprentice, and work their way up the ladder in a GM's office. I cannot comment on the relative merits of either course; each can be equally effective.

If one is thinking of pursuing a career in general management, it is helpful to be clear on what personality traits will prove useful. In common with any other form of management—stage, company, or house—a general manager has to be organized, thorough, calm, and an excellent communicator. A good rule of thumb is you have to be someone who enjoys rolling up his or her sleeves and making order out of chaos. Due to the specific nature of the job, a GM should additionally have a good head for numbers and be an effective negotiator. If this profile does not match well with your own, you should reconsider if general management is the best niche for you in the theater. It's important to play to one's strengths, not struggle against them. When I decided to make the switch from acting to management, I felt like a fish that had finally been placed in water.

In my case, once I did decide to make this change, I sought a position in a general manager's office rather than going to a graduate school. I had heard that a well-known GM had two new shows opening within a short time span and was looking to hire a second assistant.

NOTE: The production period, when a new show is being mounted, tends to be the busiest and most labor-intensive period in the life of a show. This is the time theatrical offices are most likely to hire additional staff, especially at the entry level. Find out which shows are gearing up to go into rehearsal and who is general managing them, and contact those offices about possible job openings. Even consider a short-term internship, as that can be a way of getting one's foot in the door. An excellent publication for researching this information is *Theatrical Index*, the invaluable weekly guide to what's going on in the commercial theater. It will always report who the key players are on a given project and list the contact information for such personnel as the producer, general manager, and press agent. *Theatrical Index* is available online or at such places as the Drama Book Shop.

I contacted this office and scheduled an interview, which seemed to go well. I was told that a decision would be made within the week. When a week had passed and I had not heard back, I called to inquire. The assistant who answered sounded extremely harried, told me the GM was on another call, and was not able to speak to me at this time. As soon as I hung up, I remembered a quote of Katharine Hepburn's I had once read— "Never call or write when you can go in person." Heeding her sage advice, I got up and headed straight over to the GM's office. As I stood in his open office doorway, I could see that phones were ringing off the hook. The GM happened to glance up, saw me, and said, "Thank goodness! When can you start?" "Right now," I replied. And I sat down at an empty desk, answered a phone, and stayed for half a decade.

In my experience, and that of most of my colleagues, the majority of Broadway GMs start out in entry-level positions in a GM's office and slowly work themselves up the ranks, making themselves invaluable, gaining experience and knowledge on the job, and being entrusted with increasing levels of responsibility along the way. This path is similar to starting in the mailroom of a corporation. I began as the second assistant, eventually became the first assistant, then the office manager, and finally an associate GM. But the biggest development in my journey occurred when I became actively involved in the area of company management.

Each show has its own **company manager (CM)**, an extremely responsible union position under the jurisdiction of **ATPAM**, an acronym for the **Association of Theatrical Press Agents and Managers**. The company manager is heavily involved in the day-to-day administration of the company and comes on board shortly before rehearsals are due to begin—he or she will read all the contracts, set up, calculate, and call in the weekly payroll, pay bills as directed, oversee house seat requests, make sure that union benefits are paid and sent to the appropriate fund office, enclose with them explicit cover sheets detailing what contribution should be credited to which individual's account, keep track of ticket sales and advise which performances or price sections are weak and need attention, review the weekly theater settlement that accompanies the show's settlement check, checking all the back-up as well as the arithmetic, send out royalty statements along with cover sheets and accounting statements, and submit new pricing information, performance schedule changes, or discount code requests to the box office. On top of all these office duties, the company manager must arrive at the theater an hour or so before each performance, eight shows a week, to serve as the producer and management's onsite representative, checking in with the cast and crew, making them feel valued and cared for, answering questions, handling problems, picking up company house seat orders, and, once the performance has begun, meticulously checking the accuracy of the box office statement prepared by the theater's treasurer before signing it on behalf of the producer, thereby attesting to its accuracy. These are just some of the main duties. A company manager deals with a myriad of other important details every day, six days a week. He or she needs to be equally adept at math and at people skills. In my opinion, company managers are the hardest working and the most underappreciated people in theater.

I began by asking our company manager if she needed any help. Company managers can always use help—to review the backup and check the math of someone's expense reimbursements, to stuff, address, stamp, and seal a mailing to investors, to assign house seats, to set up file folders, "etc., etc., and so forth," as the King in *The King and I* is wont to say. I read every document, budget, and contract in the office I could lay my hands on, made notes about things I didn't understand, and asked questions about them at an appropriate time. I also asked the company manager if there were ever a time I could come to the theater and trail her without being in the way. There was, but not until after the company had settled in and gotten to know her. After doing this several times, and after her clearing it with the GM, I occasionally covered a Saturday matinee for her, allowing her a little more time with her family. Ultimately, and this was the single biggest step forward, I asked the office to sponsor me for ATPAM's apprentice manager program, which would, eventually, qualify me to become an ATPAM company manager, earn a union-dictated base salary considerably higher than the average nonunion, office assistant salary, and receive pension, health, and annuity contributions from my employer. Just being a union apprentice, at 50 percent of the Broadway base, instantly doubled my income! (As a point of comparison, office assistants might make $500 a week, an ATPAM apprentice could make roughly $1,000 a week, and the current ATPAM Broadway manager minimum, at the time of writing, is $2,062 a week).

Once accepted into the program (again, one has to be sponsored by a theatrical office to be eligible), one becomes a Non-Member Apprentice Manager (NMAM; affectionately referred to as a "No, Ma'am") and may be employed as an apprentice on a show when an existing member is hired per the Minimum Basic Agreement (MBA) between ATPAM and the Broadway League. A contract for the NMAM must be filed by the employer, and at the same time as the contract filing, the NMAM must pay a nonrefundable registration fee of $250 (which will be credited toward his or her initiation fee of $2,000). To be eligible for membership in the Union, NMAM candidates must accumulate a minimum of fifty-two credit weeks on valid contracts over a period of not less than two, but no more than three, consecutive seasons. (The exact dates of a theatrical season vary slightly from year to year, but they always begin on a Monday close to Memorial Day and extend until the Sunday fifty-two weeks later). No fewer than ten credit weeks, and no more than forty-two, may be accumulated in each season. During the course of the apprenticeship, the union sponsors a series of invaluable seminars on a variety of pertinent, complex subjects. Topics may include insurance, road (touring) settlements, local stagehands versus traveling stagehands, box office statements, musicians, the front-of-house unions on Broadway, etc. For each seminar attended, the NMAM will receive a $100 credit toward the ATPAM initiation fee of $2,000 (capped at $1,000). If one fails to accumulate the required number of work weeks within three consecutive seasons, one is removed from the program. Finally, following the accumulation of fifty-two credit weeks, all NMAMs must pass a strenuous and comprehensive written and oral exam for union admission. Similar to how lawyers prepare for their bar exam, apprentices study for months to prepare for this exam, often forming study groups with fellow NMAMs to help review all the contracts and rulebooks that will be on the test. Twenty-six years later, I am still in touch with many people from my old study group, so bonded did we become as survivors of this arduous experience. The full-day final exam was so intense that I know one colleague who can still recall exactly what she had for lunch during the break between the morning and afternoon sessions!

After passing the ATPAM entrance exam, I worked for several general managers as a company manager, both on and Off Broadway, for nine years. During this time I gained a wealth of experience managing a variety of shows in a range of theaters and benefited greatly from observing, and being mentored by, multiple GMs, each with his or her own distinctive management style. However, a company manager is tied to a show schedule, has to be at the theater eight times a week, evenings and weekends, and works six days a week. Eventually I married, had a son, and wanted a more conventional Monday through Friday, 10 a.m. to 6 p.m. job with weekends off. Also, I was itching to take on greater responsibility and wanted more say in the operating of a show. The solution: find someone who knew and trusted me and was willing to give me the opportunity to be his or her GM. In time, the opportunity arose and I grabbed it.

NOTE: When one is offered the opportunity to serve as the general manager of a Broadway show, one also becomes eligible to join the Broadway League, the producers' and theater owners' collective bargaining agent and the all-around trade organization serving the Broadway community. This in turn makes one eligible to become a Tony Award® voter, a very prestigious and highly coveted position within the industry.

Like most positions in the commercial theater, general managers work on a freelance basis. When the show closes (usually at *their* financial recommendation!), they are unemployed along with the actors, stage managers, stagehands, et al. But a GM's involvement in putting together a show is so great and time consuming, GMs customarily demand, and get, right of first refusal to manage any future productions of the show under the producer's control, lease, or license, especially in North America (see chapter 8). If the show is going to have a sit-down production in a foreign city—for example, London—it is likely a local GM who knows all the customs and players will have to be hired.

Once a producer has complete trust in a GM, he tends to keep returning to that GM with future projects. It's a kind of marriage, and to paraphrase Rodgers and Hammerstein's *South Pacific*, "Once you have found him (or her, as the case may be), never let him go."

Broadway is an industry built heavily on relationships and reputation. And for a GM, his reputation is everything. As Shakespeare, in *Othello*, says:

Good name in man and woman, dear my lord,
Is the immediate jewel of their souls:
Who steals my purse steals trash; 'tis something, nothing;
'Twas mine, 'tis his, and has been slave to thousands;
But he that filches from me my good name
Robs me of that which not enriches him
And makes me poor indeed.

—*Othello*, act III, scene 3

2

The Production Budget

Traditionally, the first thing a producer does after acquiring the rights to a property is hire a general manager to prepare two different budgets—a **production budget,** which tells the producer how much money he or she needs to raise to mount the show and get it to the first paid public performance (the show's **capitalization**), and an **operating budget,** which details the costs to run the show on a weekly basis and provides various scenarios for recouping (earning back) the show's production costs.

These two budgets are only *estimates* of expenses and will be revised many times in an ongoing dialogue between the general manager and producer as new information affecting costs arises. Together, they will form the economic blueprint for the production. Once all the numbers have been calculated, one can assess if this initial business plan is indeed sound or if it needs to be adjusted. For example, if a show's breakeven (explained further in chapter 3 and in the glossary, but for those who can't wait, the box office gross at which the show's revenue just covers its running costs, leaving neither profit nor loss) turns out to be too high, one should consider several options—reducing costs, raising ticket prices, booking a larger theater—to achieve a better balance between revenue and cost.

For the purposes of illustration, sample budgets for a Broadway play with the following arbitrary parameters appear at the end of this chapter on page 42: five sets, twelve actors (including understudies; three of the twelve are stars, two of whom do not live in New York City), and slated to go into a Broadway theater of roughly 1,000 seats. In general, plays are simpler to budget than musicals, not having the additional musical departments required by a musical. But the basic principals are the same. The attached budgets, when appropriate, reflect the union minimums, or percentages thereof, as of this writing.

NOTE: It is important to stress that the cost of various items and services, equipment rentals, and minimum union salaries changes every year; the figures given in this book, while accurate at the time of writing, are intended to convey the concepts that go into budgeting. The numbers themselves are not meant to be taken as absolute cost guidelines and should not be appropriated by a nonprofessional who is attempting to cobble together his own budget.

Good budgeting begins with a careful reading of the script and the knowledge of how to analyze the text from a financial point of view. For example, how many scenes of varying location are specified in the script, how much time elapses between scenes or acts, is it a period piece or set in the present, and what is the age range and ethnicity of the male and female characters? The answers to these questions, along with discussions with key artistic personnel, will give the general manager valuable guidance for budgeting the cost of the set design, determining the basis for negotiating the designers' fees, calculating the crew size needed to operate the show, quantifying the costume budget, estimating the number of people required in the wardrobe and hair departments, and judging how many understudies should be hired to cover all roles! Every play is unique, and a thorough reading of a script will also reveal if one should budget for any special needs—for example, a dialect coach, fight director, special effects designer, make-up designer, dance consultant, child wrangler, or tutor.

While no two individuals organize their budgets in exactly the same way, budgets are divided into basic predictable categories, each of which in turn has numerous subcategories. Starting with the attached production budget, items will be reviewed line by line.

Before starting, it should be noted that every production budget is comprised of three basic components—productions costs, advances/bonds/deposits, and a reserve. The **production costs**, which comprise the majority of the total capitalization, are those expenses that one expects to have spent by the first paid public performance. In the attached budget, they comprise $2,760,000 out of the total capitalization of $3,500,000. Advances, bonds, and deposits—to the author, director, designers, theatrical unions, and the theater, plus possibly for star housing—are considered from an accounting point of view to be assets or recoverables rather than expenses. An advance is a partial prepayment of the initial weekly compensation a creative will receive once the show starts operating. It is a way of both giving the creative additional money upfront beyond just her fee and allowing the producer to account for that payment as an advance against operating expenses, so the payment does not increase the show's production costs. If a show closes before all of an advance has been worked off, any unused portion converts to a closing expense.

NOTE: An advance against royalties is "worked off" each week by calculating the royalty the individual would have received if he or she didn't have an advance and reducing the value of the advance, which is essentially a credit, by the amount of that calculation. At the point where there is no credit or partial credit remaining, the royalty recipient begins receiving a royalty payment again. Only calculations above minimum guarantees can be used to reduce the advance; the minimum guarantees themselves are not applicable.

Finally, the reserve is additional money that is budgeted to subsidize losses during previews and early post-opening weeks. Most shows take longer to catch on than their producers imagine, and a healthy reserve is the key to whether a show can hang in and find its audience (i.e., advertise and market effectively so as to reach its initial core audience, which will vary depending on such variables as whether the show appeals to young or old, Manhattanites or suburbanites, etc.) or not. The determination whether or not the amount budgeted for a reserve is truly adequate cannot be made until after the general manager has completed the operating budget and fully understands how much it will cost to run the show. If a producer cannot raise all the money to adequately produce a show, including a substantial reserve to protect the money that will be spent on production costs, it would be wise to abandon the project.

My personal philosophy of budgeting is to budget realistically but conservatively. The GM is perceived as a hero if the show comes in under budget and a schmuck if it comes in over!

PHYSICAL PRODUCTION
This category contains all the physical elements—sets, props, costumes, wigs, lights, sound—of the show. See page 42 to view this production budget.

SCENERY ($425,000)
This is one of the most expensive individual line items in a budget. The figure here represents an amount for a realistic, fairly detailed, multiple set for a Broadway play. This is also one of the hardest items to budget and requires considerable experience. Sometimes a producer wants an initial budget before a director and set designer are on board, making it particularly difficult to anticipate the vision they will have for physically realizing the play.

Once the initial scenic design has been reviewed and approved by the director, technical supervisor, producer, and GM, the technical supervisor and designer will confer on which scenic shops should be invited to bid on the show. It is pointless to invite any shop the designer has previously had a bad experience with or one that does not have a good reputation within the industry. As in all areas, multiple bids are normally solicited. At a bid session, the designer makes a presentation to the invited scenic shops, demonstrating all the scene changes on a detailed, scale set model, reviewing each page of the accompanying blueprints, and pointing out details for the shops to take special note of along the way. The shops then go away, do their calculations, and send in written, itemized bids for the job, responding by a previously specified deadline. The lowest bid, taking all other variables into account such as past experience and how many other projects the shop has already committed to for the same time period, is awarded the contract. Sometimes even the lowest bid will come in over budget, and the designer and technical director will then have to come up with design modifications, or cuts, that are acceptable to them, the director, and the producer. In this instance, the common wisdom is to keep as much downstage center as possible and cut elements that are upstage and on the periphery! Savvy designers will have included elements in the design that they would like to see on stage, cost permitting, but are prepared to lose if cuts are required.

NOTE: As a GM, it is important to remember that everyone has an agenda and secretly (or perhaps not so secretly!) wants to advance his or her career. I once GM'd a show, a thriller, where the main action was set in a cabin in the woods, in which a woman, who was being stalked by a psychotic killer, was trapped alone during a snowstorm. Even though the cabin was described as having two levels, which figured prominently in the denouement, the set should have conveyed a sense of claustrophobia that added to the tension. We had a very talented designer on the show, who came up with a stunning design the producer fell in love with. "It's a clap trap!" the producer cried upon seeing the set model, meaning, as soon as the curtain rose, the audience would spontaneously burst into applause. And they did. Problem was, this grand, beautiful set was really more of a lodge than a cabin! In hindsight, who did the design serve more—the playwright or the designer?

AUTOMATION ($25,000)

In this example, there are five distinct, realistic locations, so it is likely some automation will be required for scenery to track on and off stage and help transitions to flow seamlessly.

PROPS/DRESSING ($25,000)

This category covers the furniture, appliances, and set dressing—books, paintings, lamps, rugs, tchotchkes—that are placed on the set but not actually constructed by a scenic shop. Again, the amount indicated here is for a fairly detailed, realistic, ordinary, contemporary design, not an elaborate period set, or a minimal abstract one, or one that is supposed to give the impression of great wealth.

REHEARSAL PROPS/SCENERY ($7,500)

Certain prop items and scenic elements may need to be made available to the actors in the rehearsal hall. Sometimes rehearsal props can be the actual items that will be used in the theater. More often, facsimiles of key scenic elements (for example, stairs, a bed, a refrigerator, kitchen cabinets) are mocked up for the rehearsal period and will need to be designed, constructed, and shipped to and from the rehearsal hall.

DRESSING ROOM COSTS ($7,500)

Especially where stars are concerned, a producer should be prepared to have a budget to spruce up the star dressing room(s) with a new coat of paint and to provide certain amenities that are traditionally agreed to in a star's contract—a half refrigerator, humidifier, private telephone, new sofa big enough to nap on between shows, drapes and throw cushions, an arm chair, etc. Often it is cheaper to rent some of these items than to buy them, depending on the anticipated length of the run. Most Broadway dressing rooms are surprisingly small and dingy, and even if they come with their own internal bathrooms, as is customary for those assigned to stars, those bathrooms tend to be very basic.

NOTE: Yul Brynner, the original star of the aforementioned *The King and I*, was legendary for the excessive demands he placed on producers for the outfitting of both his dressing room and his hotel room, especially when he went on tour. Each dressing room he occupied had to be painted a particular shade of brown (and restored to its original, neutral color as soon as he vacated). In addition, he demanded a refrigerator be installed and stocked with explicitly detailed food and beverage—including one dozen brown eggs (had to be brown, white eggs were unacceptable) and a case of Chateau Gruaud Larose '66, the only wine he would drink. He even went so far as to specify the length of the telephone cords that had to be in his rooms—thirteen feet long, exactly!

COSTUMES ($40,000)

This figure will reflect how many costumes are needed (how many actors, how many scenes, how much time has elapsed between scenes), whether the costumes are contemporary or period, and whether they can primarily be bought off the rack, rented from a costume shop, or need to be custom made. Also, do the costumes need to give the impression of belonging to ordinary people or to society swells? All these variables go into estimating this number.

HAIR/MAKE-UP ($9,000)

Will any of the actors wear wigs? Can they be store bought and made of synthetic fibers, or do they need to be custom made from real human hair and lace-fronted, designed by one of Broadways top wig makers? Are there any unusual make-up demands that need to be designed and/or built, such as Cyrano's nose? Sometimes you don't know the answers to these questions when you are preparing the budget, so it is wise to set a little something aside in this category as a precaution. This is a modest sum and covers two custom-made quality wigs, a few rental items and hairpieces, including a mustache, and some basic make-up for three stars.

ELECTRICS ($16,500)

This is an upfront cost, or guarantee, for the first three weeks of expenses to the electrics shop that is supplying the lighting equipment. It represents all payments to the shop for equipment rental from the time the equipment leaves the shop up until the first paid public performance. From that point onward, a lower weekly rental should be contained within the operating budget.

Once the lighting designer has drafted his lighting plot and an equipment list has been drawn up, the technical supervisor, working in coordination with the GM's office, sends out bids to interested shops (just like for the scenic and sound designs).

CARPENTRY/ELECTRICS/SOUND (PERISHABLES) ($15,000)

This figure accounts for "perishable" items (i.e., items that have a finite life, will get used up, and will need to be replaced) such as masking tape for marking the stage, colored gel for the lights, lighting templates that cast specific images on the stage, light bulbs, batteries, rope for rigging, flash lights, and the basic hardware supplies that are needed for the installation of the physical production.

SOUND (PREPARATION) ($7,500)

This accounts for the initial sound equipment rental guarantee and, as with lights, represents payment from the time the equipment loads out of the shop until the first paid public performance. Thereafter, the rental is accounted for in the weekly operating budget. This figure represents a modest amount for a straight play (as distinct from a musical) with minimal sound needs.

SOUND (RECORDING) ($10,000)

This figure accounts for studio recording time and editing of any sound effects and/or incidental music that need to be recorded for performances. While some effects may be done live, others may need to be prerecorded and cued. If the script indicates sirens, thunder, birdcalls, or people listening to a television or radio program, chances are some studio time will be required to create a recording.

NOTE: While many sound cues are recorded, like the ringing of a doorbell or telephone, those cues are still called and executed by live people, leaving plenty of room for human error. Remember that thriller referred to under "Scenery"? It ended with a sound cue—the star, alone onstage, pressed the button on a small tape recorder, and a surprise message was heard that ended the show. We were out of town on a pre-Broadway tryout, it was the first preview, and the producer and I were sitting in the last row of the Orchestra, nervously watching the performance. It had been a difficult day, with last min-ute, problematic technical rehearsals right up until half hour (before the show begins), but, so far, things had gone surpris-ingly smoothly. Just a few minutes left, and we could all heave a huge sigh of relief. The big moment arrived, our star pressed the button—and nothing happened. She pressed it again and still no cue. The producer and I leaned forward in our seats, our mouths agape, mesmerized. We watched as it became pain-fully clear to our star that this cue was never going to come, and unless she ad-libbed something fast, she would not be able to exit the stage. People always speak of the magic of live theater, rarely of the horrors. Luckily, our star was quick on her feet and came up with something (I have mercifully blotted out what she managed to babble forth in her terror), and the curtain did fall. As did the head of the sound operator shortly thereafter.

FEES

This category comprises fee payments for various personnel, mostly artis-tic, some of whom will receive no other compensation beyond this and some of whom, once the show begins operating, will receive additional weekly royalties, either in the form of fixed amounts or as varying percent-ages of the box office gross or of net operating profits.

AUTHOR ($0)

The author normally receives an option payment in exchange for granting the producer the exclusive rights, within a specific territory or territories and for a specified period of time, to produce the show, usually with pre-negotiated extension periods contingent upon the payment of additional sums. On Broadway, this option fee can be credited as an advance against royalties, recoupable once the show has earned back its production costs. Because of this, nothing appears here under fees for the author, but this fee, plus an advance, is accounted for under "Advances, Bonds, and Deposits" toward the end of the budget.

Director ($50,000)

This is an over-scale (i.e., above union minimum) amount, payable to an in-demand, successful Broadway director with multiple Broadway credits. On Broadway, directors' contracts are subject to the collective bargaining agreement bilaterally negotiated between the **Broadway League** (representing producers and theater owners) and the **Stage Directors and Choreographers Society, Inc.** (SDC). Minimum fee and advance payments are specified in the agreement, although nothing prevents an agent from negotiating for better terms for his or her client.

Executive Producer ($35,000)

A fee, intended to partially compensate the lead producer(s) for an extensive development period of a project during which time he or she received no compensation for his or her efforts. This period could last for several years.

General Manager ($32,500)

This is the GM's production fee and represents all the compensation the GM receives from the point of engagement up until several weeks prior to the start of rehearsals (often two weeks). This fee is traditionally paid in several installments, the first on the signing of the GM's agreement, one or two upon negotiated thresholds along the way, and the balance at the point several weeks prior to the start of rehearsal when the GM's weekly compensation begins. As previously noted, this production period could last several years.

Scenic Designer ($13,217)

This represents the current (at the time of writing) minimum fee for a multi-set play agreed upon by the designers' collective bargaining agent, **United Scenic Artists** (USA), and the Broadway League, representing producers and theater owners. Different minimum fees and advances are stated for different categories of scenic design—whether it is a single set (all the action takes place in someone's living room), a multi-set (the first act occurs in a living room, the second act is set in a Chinese restaurant), or a unit set with phases—one basic set that is always visible with different playing areas delineated on it, the action at any given time taking place in only one lighted area. Perhaps anticipating that a cost-conscious producer (is there any other kind?) will try to push for that last category, which should be cheaper to build, USA has negotiated a higher fee and advance payment for a unit set with phases than for a multi-set design! It is therefore important to try to determine accurately what the category of set design is likely to be when budgeting a show. The amount budgeted here is the required minimum, the assumption being that the designer to be hired is relatively young, has mostly regional theater credits, has not won any significant industry awards, and is probably a newcomer to Broadway. In short, this engagement will represent a major career break for the designer, and his agent should not expect to get over-scale compensation, though that won't necessarily stop him from trying!

COSTUME DESIGNER ($9,920)
This figure reflects the current (at the time of writing) USA minimum for the category of one to fifteen characters, plus an additional period supplement for the same number of characters, as the play is not set in the present.

LIGHTING DESIGNER ($9,915)
This figure reflects the current (at the time of writing) USA minimum for the lighting design of a multi-set play.

SOUND DESIGNER ($7,500)
This figure is a little higher than the current USA minimum for sound designers (at the time of writing). The amount of the designer's fee should reflect how extensive the sound design of the play is and how experienced the sound designer is.

WIG DESIGNER ($5,000)
This is a modest creative fee for the designer, separate from the cost of the actual wigs (see "Hair/Make-Up" on page 42). It covers a fee for two custom-made, lace-fronted wigs made from human hair.

COMPOSER ($7,500)
This fee is for the composing of incidental music, played as the lights dim at the top of the show, between scenes to cover set transitions, at the end of

Act I when lights go to black or the curtain falls, at the end of intermission as the second act begins, between scenes where set transitions occur, during curtain call, and as exit music. All in all, the total amount of incidental music used will probably not exceed fifteen minutes.

TECHNICAL SUPERVISOR
(OFTEN ABBREVIATED AS TECH SUPERVISOR) ($18,000)

This is the individual who oversees all the technical aspects of the show—arranges production meetings with all departments; reviews the drafted set, lighting, and sound designs before they go out for bidding; coordinates the bid sessions for these elements; works with the designers to come up with design modifications if the bids come in over budget; determines the number of stagehands needed to load in and install the set, lights, sound, props, and costumes; supervises the load-in and load-out of the show; recommends qualified individuals for any needed production crew positions (for example, sound board operator, production props, or light board operator); arranges for trucking; makes sure the production meets all fire department codes and that all flammable physical production elements have been professionally flame-proofed; and sees to it that there are certificates on hand at the theater testifying to that effect when the fire department inspects the premises prior to the first paid public performance.

NOTE: Safety rules exist for good reason. The requirement that all potentially flammable physical production elements be flame-proofed, that the show have certificates from a licensed shop attesting to this, and that a local fire chief come to the theater and personally test the objects did not always exist. As the author Shauna Vey recounts in her excellent book *Childhood and Nineteenth-Century American Theatre*, in 1859, eleven-year-old Little Mary Marsh, one of the most famous juvenile actors in America, suffered a horrible death in Macon, Georgia, when she wandered too close to the candle-lit footlights and her costume burst into flames on stage. She died the next day.

Sometimes, the crew department heads that come with the house (theater) (carpentry, props, electrics) are able to staff all the show's technical needs and are paid additional weekly production fees for fulfilling the show's needs as well as the theater's. More often than not, the show hires some of its own **IATSE** (an acronym for **International Alliance of Theatrical Stage Employees**) crew members, who are solely dedicated to operating and maintaining the show's technical needs. In reference to the color of their contracts, these production stagehands are called **Pinks**, as compared to the Local One stagehands who work for the theater. Pinks are paid on the show's payroll, while Local One stagehands are paid on the theater's payroll and their salaries (plus payroll taxes and benefits) are charged back to the production as part of the weekly theater settlement. Sometimes a technical supervisor is affiliated with the scenic shop who will construct the scenery, and it is possible to get a break on this fee because the shop knows it is going to be awarded a contract worth hundreds of thousands of dollars.

PRESS PREPRODUCTION ($7,500)
This is a sum of money to cover the press agent's occasional preproduction input/involvement in the show prior to going on an official union (**ATPAM**) contract. The sum should reflect the scope of work anticipated and the length of time it is meant to cover—six months, nine months, etc.

MARKETING CONSULTANT ($7,500)
Comparable to press preproduction above—a lump sum for marketing people to begin part-time work on the show, prior to going on a weekly retainer as the start of rehearsals approaches. A marketing consultant traditionally designs, builds, and maintains the show's website, handles online marketing and social media campaigns, and looks for places where the show can have an advantageous presence—at a trade convention, in the window of a prestigious department store, in prominent signage, etc.

CASTING DIRECTOR ($18,000)
A casting director draws up lists of actors for all roles and understudy assignments, sends out a character breakdown to talent agents, arranges for

required **Actors' Equity Association** (**AEA** or **Equity**, the union for actors and stage managers) Principal Interviews, required by Equity so that their members have an opportunity to be seen for a show, and schedules actors to audition for the director and producer(s). Experienced casting directors know how to get a script to a star, who is available and who is not, who is known to have substance abuse problems and should be avoided, who wants to work with another actor, who is having an affair with another actor, who has had an affair with another actor and is no longer speaking to that person, etc.! A casting director's fee will normally reflect how much work is anticipated: how many characters, how many understudies, how many stars, how many interviews to schedule, and whether or not a major talent hunt involving travel to other cities or even countries is planned. The amount in this budget takes all of these factors into account for a play with twelve actors—four large speaking roles, four small speaking roles, and four understudies. The fee should also reflect how active the director and producer will be in suggesting actors themselves.

DIALECT COACH ($5,000)

This position may or may not be needed. The fee will reflect how much work is expected—how many actors to work with and how many hours of coaching they will require. Sometimes a coach is needed to teach an accent or dialect. Sometimes, especially if an actor does not have much stage experience, a coach is needed to teach an actor how to project on stage and use his or her voice correctly without straining it.

MAKE-UP CONSULTANT ($3,000)

As with a dialect coach, this position may or may not be needed. Important things to consider—does the script indicate special make-up needs in the show, like a prosthetic nose (think Cyrano again), scars, bruises, whip lashes, aging? Sometimes actors just need to be trained to execute a make-up design and then can do the work themselves; sometimes, the make-up is of such a scope it requires a make-up department to apply it, necessitating their addition to the show's running crew. Also, stars, particularly those with the majority of their experience in film or television, may be used to a professional make-up artist applying their make-up and may insist on someone doing it for them at every performance.

ASSISTANT SCENIC DESIGNER ($8,964)

Most set designers require at least one assistant to help them do research, build a set model (although more and more this is being replaced by computerized, digital renderings), draft detailed scale blueprints from which the scene shop will construct the sets, and supervise the load-in of the scenery at the theater. The number of weeks an assistant is needed will vary depending on the complexity of the set, how busy the designer is, and whether or not the show is playing an out-of-town engagement (requiring its own load-in) prior to the set's installation in the New York theater. This sum represents the current (at time of writing) United Scenic Artists minimum weekly design assistant rate for a period of six weeks.

ASSISTANT COSTUME DESIGNER ($8,964)

An assistant costume designer may be involved with research, shopping, returning items, supervising fittings, and compiling the costume department's paperwork—the budgets, the costume "bible" detailing each character's costume plot (a scene-by-scene breakdown of what each character is wearing, including shoes, hat, gloves, and jewelry, if applicable), and the submission of (organized!) expense receipts for reimbursement. The number of costumes needed and whether or not they can be purchased or will have to be custom made will clearly impact how many weeks an assistant is needed. This sum represents the current (at time of writing) United Scenic Artists minimum weekly design assistant rate for a period of six weeks.

ASSISTANT LIGHTING DESIGNER ($8,964)

Similar concerns to assistant scenic designer and assistant costume designer.

ASSISTANT SOUND DESIGNER ($7,470)

Most plays tend to have fairly basic sound designs. This sum represents the current (at time of writing) United Scenic Artists minimum weekly design assistant rate for a period of five weeks.

ASSISTANT DIRECTOR (AD) ($7,500)

In their contract negotiation, most directors will require an **assistant director** (**AD**) who will work closely with them and take notes from the first day of rehearsal, if not one week prior to that date, through all rehearsals, tech, and previews, up to opening night. An AD is normally paid a weekly amount and, despite the name here, serves more as an assistant *to* the director. This sum represents a weekly rate of $750 for a period of ten weeks. The weekly amount is modest and presupposes a young assistant, previously unknown to the director, thrilled to experience firsthand the process of mounting a Broadway show and attending a Broadway opening night. This is very different from someone who has worked with the director previously, who the director has requested, and who may actually function as an assistant director rather than as an assistant to the director! It is important to consult the director and be clear what level of assistant he or she is expecting.

Prop Shopper ($15,000)

This is for a person who will work closely with the designer to acquire all the furniture and set dressing that appear on stage. Obviously, the rate will vary depending on the scope of the work required—number of scenes, amount of realistic detail in each scene, estimated number of hours spent shopping, etc. Prop shoppers often search for items, take digital photos of what they have found, and clear the items with the set designer and director before they purchase them and have them delivered to the theater.

Production Assistant (PA) ($9,000)

Usually a runner or gofer (as in "Go for this, go for that!"). A **production assistant** (**PA**) may be needed in the general manager's office, as well as in the rehearsal room to assist the stage managers. Usually, a nominal weekly fee or salary is paid to a PA in exchange for the opportunity to observe and participate in the process of mounting a show from first rehearsal to opening night. This sum represents two PAs, for an average of ten weeks at a weekly rate of $450 each. Recent legislation requires that the payment for these individuals meet minimum wage standards.

Miscellaneous Roles

Other categories that could be needed for a play but do not apply to every show include a fight director, a special effects designer (primarily rain, snow, or fire), an animal trainer, a tutor, and a child wrangler, among others. Of course, musicals will require a battery of additional musical personnel—orchestrator, arranger (for vocal, dance, incidental, and/or transitional music), contractor, copyist, musical director, choreographer and assistant(s), moving lights programmer, synth programmer, etc.

REHEARSAL/TECH SALARIES

A play typically rehearses in a rehearsal hall or studio separate from the theater for about four weeks. (Musicals, especially those with a chorus and extensive choreography, require several more weeks of rehearsal). During the latter part of this time, the pipes needed to hang the scenery, lighting, and sound equipment are rigged (put in place) in the theater, some of the lighting and sound equipment, specifically those instruments hung over the stage, are prehung on the pipes, and finally, the remainder of the lighting and sound equipment, as well as the scenery, is loaded into the theater. Once all is installed, the actors move from the rehearsal hall to the theater and "tech" the show prior to being able to do run-throughs and begin paid public performances. During the tech period, lighting and sound cue levels are set, technical cues are written into the stage manager's script so the stage manager can call them during a performance, scene change transitions between scenes are rehearsed over and over, costume quick changes are worked through, etc. The amount of time needed for the tech period varies depending on the complexity of the scenic, lighting, sound, and costume designs. This section contains the salaries of the company—cast, crew, and administration—over the rehearsal and tech period. Once the show begins performances (i.e., is operating), these salaries are contained in the weekly operating budget and, some, particularly those of key actors, may increase.

STARS ($40,270)

This show anticipates four stars for five weeks of combined rehearsal/tech at the Actors' Equity Association (AEA, or Equity, the union for actors and stage managers), production contract (for Broadway), current (at time of writing!) minimum weekly, plus an additional **Media Payment**, typically 2 percent of the current actor minimum, approximately $39. This media payment allows producers the right to record the show, in whole or in part, and use this footage for a wide variety of noncommercial, advertising, and marketing purposes to promote the show, where no income is earned by its use. Outlets for this footage include the show's own website, talk shows where members of the cast appear, or television news programs that do a feature on the show or review the show. Prior to beginning paid public performances, the industry standard is for all actors, including stars, to be paid contractual minimum. Of course, during this period, stars may also receive additional perks such as housing and per diem if they do not live locally, car service to and from the rehearsal hall or theater, and security.

PRINCIPALS ($40,270)

These are your nonstar actors with speaking roles. All the actors, even their understudies, must be, or become, members of Equity. The salary amount of this line item reflects four principals, at time of writing, minimum plus Media Payment over a five-week period of rehearsal/tech.

UNDERSTUDIES ($40,270)

It is important to check with the producer and director *when* they wish the understudies to begin their employment. Equity does not require understudies to be hired until two weeks after the first public performance. However, if one waits until that point to hire (and rehearse) understudies and someone gets sick before then, a performance may have to be cancelled, which can be costly. Also, if the understudies do not start until after previews have begun, they will not have reaped the benefit of sitting in the rehearsal room and hearing the director give notes to the cast as their roles are developed. Thus different factors, or even philosophies, may dictate when understudies are expected to begin their employment. If, at the time of initial budgeting, it has not been decided when the understudies will be asked to begin rehearsals, it is wise, as here, to budget them for the full rehearsal period and, if the director ultimately decides to have them start later, realize a savings. Chances are good that savings will wind up being applied to a cost overrun elsewhere! The figure here represents four understudies, whose employment begins as of the first week of rehearsal.

STAGE MANAGERS ($36,537)

On Broadway, Equity requires that for a play, the head stage manager, referred to as the **production stage manager** (PSM), be hired two weeks before the start of rehearsals and an **assistant stage manager** (ASM) be hired one week prior to the start of rehearsals. In addition, all stage managers must be paid an additional one-sixth of their weekly salary during the tech week prior to the start of previews. Top, in-demand stage managers usually receive more than minimum and are well worth every penny they are paid. This figure reflects all these variables and allows for a PSM at $150/week above minimum.

PRODUCERS ($26,250)
Often producers receive a weekly executive producer fee, in addition to an office fee (which is meant to help defray their real office expenses) and a royalty (which is frequently the first expense to get waived or deferred when a show is losing money). Along with an office fee, this payment frequently begins two weeks prior to the start of rehearsals. This figure represents $3,750/week for seven weeks (starting two weeks prior to five weeks of rehearsal/tech).

GENERAL MANAGER (GM) ($22,750)
Traditionally, a GM goes on salary two weeks prior to the first rehearsal and is retained until two weeks after the final performance. This figure represents seven weeks of salary at $3,250/week.

COMPANY MANAGER (CM) ($16,821)
On Broadway, company managers, press agents, and house managers are members of the **Association of Theatrical Press Agents and Managers** (**ATPAM**). Without applying to ATPAM for any concessions, the standard employment of the company manager is required to begin four weeks prior to the week of the first paid public performance. If, however, that date coincides with the first day of rehearsal, it is wise to start the CM a week or two before then—there is just too much information and too many contracts for the company manager to read and absorb and too many things for him or her to set up and organize before rehearsals begin. This sum represents seven weeks at $100 above the current, at time of writing, minimum, to be able to attract an experienced, in-demand manager. It also includes an extra one-sixth required premium for tech week (see comment in the previous section on Stage Managers).

PRESS AGENT ($12,565)

Analogous to the company manager, with the same start date requirements but with a slightly higher pay scale, presumably based on the fact that press agents normally bear the expense of maintaining their own office and staffs, while company managers work out of the GM's office.

WARDROBE ($15,644)

In New York, the wardrobe department is under the jurisdiction of IATSE's **Local 764**, which sets the working conditions and the pay rates for wardrobe supervisors, their assistants, and the actors' dressers. This sum represents one supervisor and two dressers, for a two-week load-in and tech period, with extensive overtime built in for the final, "**10 out of 12**" tech period, the week immediately prior to the first paid public performance, when cast and crew can be called for twelve hours from noon to midnight with two hours off for breaks.

HAIR/MAKE-UP ($4,393)

On Broadway, this department is under the jurisdiction of IATSE's **Local 798**, which sets the working conditions and the pay rates for supervisors and their assistants. Obviously the scope of the hair or make-up design for the show, if any, will determine how large this department needs to be. This figure represents one person for the tech period, plus overtime.

PINK CREW ($13,200)

This figure is for IATSE Pink contract production stagehands (in contrast to the theater's Local One [NYC] stagehands), who work directly for the show, not the theater. Every show requires a different number of crew members to meet its specific production needs. The show's technical supervisor will advise if the show needs to hire any IATSE Pink contracts (so called because of the color of their contract) and, if so, in which areas (carpentry, automation, electrics, sound, props) or if the theater's own Local One crew heads, plus possibly additional assistants, will suffice. The figure in this budget allows for two Pink contract stagehands at $2,200/week for two weeks, including overtime for the long "10 out of 12" tech days. Even on these days, when the show is allowed to rehearse from noon to midnight, there may be work calls from 8 a.m. to noon for the crew to address technical issues. For those crew members who are on both work and rehearsal calls, that means a sixteen-hour day, from 8 a.m. to midnight, which racks up a lot of overtime!

REHEARSAL/PREVIEW EXPENSES

THEATER EXPENSES ($105,000)

Those costs incurred by the show at the theater prior to the first paid public performance (excluding load-in crew expenses for installing the physical production elements, which are accounted for separately). The theater initially pays for these expenses and subsequently bills the show for their reimbursement via a detailed theater settlement with itemized backup. Theater expenses include items like payroll for box office treasurers, the house manager and porters, the stage doorman, utilities, housekeeping supplies (toilet paper, soap, light bulbs), cartage, exterminating, telephone service, remote phone sales service, and rent, usually reduced prior to paid performances, for the load-in and tech period. Obviously the decision on how early to open the box office to the public will impact these costs. Most shows find it economical to go on "soft sale" (meaning telephone and Internet sales only) much earlier than opening the theater's box office for walk-up window sales. Not only are those soft-sale weeks considerably less expensive for the show, but studies have shown that the majority of sales are now conducted via telephone and the Internet.

HALLS/THEATER ($14,000)

Covers the costs of renting a hall to hold auditions, as well as the rent for a rehearsal space for four weeks, often with a separate, small, stage manager's office attached. It is very important that the rehearsal space be equipped with, or have access to, a copier, fax machine, telephone, and answering machine. Good rehearsal space is usually in high demand and should be one of the first things secured by the general manager as soon as the show's production schedule is determined.

STAGE MANAGER AND DEPARTMENTAL ($6,000)

Consists of expense reimbursements to various company personnel such as stage managers, designers, design assistants, the casting office, and the tech director. It is surprising how these out-of-pocket expenses add up. Items covered here include transportation, long-distance telephone calls, messengers or overnight couriers, script and blueprint copying, and, in the case of stage management, setting up an office and a green room (backstage lounge for the company, often with coffee service) first in a rehearsal hall and then subsequently at the theater.

ADVERTISING AND PUBLICITY

This category traditionally should make up approximately 20 to 25 percent of the total production expenses. Although it has been divided into different line items, the exact subdivision of funds will be refined through consultation with the advertising agency, which will propose a business plan that recommends how best to allocate the budget. The final allocation is usually the result of a dialogue between the ad agency, the producer, and the general manager.

NOTE: The ad agency normally consults with the GM on how much money has been allocated for advertising in the production budget and in the weekly operating budget in order to devise its business plans. These are complicated documents, especially the initial operating plan, which may encompass the first twelve to sixteen playing weeks, and few people other than the GM rarely take the time to analyze them thoroughly. Now, numbers can be manipulated, and no one knows this better than a GM. In a proposed operating plan, the weekly expenses are usually averaged over the period of time in question, yielding an average weekly figure that is in line with the number the GM has told the ad agency is in the budget. However, since this is an average figure, in reality the early weeks in the plan often have far more allocated to them than what was budgeted, and the last few weeks often have vastly less. I understand the value of "front loading" your budget—spending disproportionately more in the beginning to try and build advance sales—and a legitimate argument can be made for doing this. However, cynically, I also recognize that if a show is not successful and closes prematurely, but the ad agency has disproportionately allocated the majority of your budget spend to the first few weeks, then even with this early closing, the agency will succeed in receiving its commission on the majority of your budget! As a GM, I feel I have to be relatively conservative in my planning. If the show turns out not to be a sold-out smash hit, sufficient funds have to be left in the budget to advertise and sell tickets for later weeks. So don't be fooled by an average weekly budget figure that looks like it is in line with the operating budget—see how it has been allocated and make sure no week in the plan has a sub-standard amount of money assigned to it.

PRINT/MEDIA ($150,000)

Accounts for all the newspaper or print advertising prior to the first preview. Traditionally, a show runs its first, relatively large display ad in the newspaper the day before the theater's box office opens. This is called an announcement ad and serves the purpose of announcing the show's existence to the general public. This initial ad often includes the billing of everyone in the company who has negotiated contractual billing—not just the author, director, producers, and cast, but also the designers, stage manager, press agent, casting agent, general manager, technical director, and advertising agency, among others. The announcement ad is followed up by ABC ads (alphabetical directory listings) and by sporadic display ads that increase in frequency as the first public performance approaches. The question of how much to initially spend on newspaper advertising prior to a show's opening and being reviewed must be weighed against how much one thinks one has to advertise—do you have a well-known author, director, or star(s)? Is the piece new, or is it a revival of a beloved classic? Often, it is decided not to overspend before opening but to reserve funds for a bigger campaign once the reviews (hopefully good!) are in hand and quotes can be pulled from them.

NOTE: Several years ago, I had the great pleasure of general managing Yasmina Reza's play *The Unexpected Man* at the Off Broadway Promenade Theatre. The play was directed by Yasmina's longtime collaborator, the brilliant English director Matthew Warchus, and starred two English acting legends, Eileen Atkins and Alan Bates. (Both shortly thereafter were made a Dame and a Sir, respectively, by Queen Elizabeth). Yasmina had recently won the Tony Award for her play *Art*, and *The Unexpected Man* had been a big hit in London. So this was a property that had five terrific angles to advertise right out of the gate—play, author, director, and two legendary English actors. We strategized our preopening ad campaign to take advantage of this, the centerpiece of which was a big direct mail campaign, and before opening had built an advance of over $1,000,000, a record at that time for an Off Broadway offering.

This category may also contain money to produce and purchase air time for a flight of radio or television spots. Again, such spots will be more effective after opening *if* one is able to quote positive reviews.

OUTDOOR ($57,500)
This is an allocation for outdoor advertising on, or in, places such as billboards, buses, commuter rail or ferry stations, the subways, telephone kiosks, etc.

DIRECT RESPONSE ($130,000)
One of the main endeavors covered here is direct mail. Even with printing, the purchasing of mailing lists of prospective patrons, and postage costs, a direct mail piece often yields one of the highest returns of any form of trackable advertising. Again, it helps if you have something to advertise—author, play, director, and/or star(s) that individually or collectively generate enough excitement to inspire a recipient to rush out and purchase tickets without waiting for the reviews. A direct mail piece traditionally offers an

incentive to buy in the form of a discount if the ticket is purchased before a certain date, often opening night, prior to the reviews being released. It is sent to a selection of carefully targeted theatergoers, who are chosen either from lists of previous ticket buyers to similar shows or from subscribers to a nonprofit theater that produces work of a similar nature.

This category also includes efforts like email blasts, which can be very cost efficient as they require no printing or postage, and digital follow ads and banner ads, which are becoming increasingly popular.

PRODUCTION/PRINTING ($105,000)
This section provides for the costs entailed in creating and reproducing the show's artwork in all its applications, such as newspaper ads or digital banner ads. It will also contain the fee for the creation of the show's logo artwork and title treatment.

FRONT OF HOUSE ($20,000)
Covers the design and production of those items that give the show a presence outside the theater—the marquee, production photos and a houseboard (similar in look to the show's title page in the *Playbill*) for display cases, underslings (signs hung below the marquee) with quotes and/or creative billing, quote panels to go on the outside of, or above, exit doors, an Equity cast board listing the company, a performance schedule, and a price scale. No two Broadway theaters are identical in the amount of "real estate" (i.e., display area) they offer the show for advertising.

MISCELLANEOUS ($15,000)
A catch-all for unusual items, such as catering and room rental for a group sales presentation, aimed at exciting group sales agents about the show so they will recommend it to their clients.

RADIO ($35,000)
An allocation to cover the production of a radio spot. This is a relatively modest initial sum, before there are reviews to quote.

WEBSITE SERVICES ($22,500)
Money to design, build, and launch the show's website.

MARKETING ($35,000)

Accounts for the cost of various marketing endeavors to help promote the play—often involving free advertising in exchange for ticket trade, discounts to special target groups, or prominently displaying a marketing sponsor in the show's advertising. Marketing endeavors may include such things as appearances at conventions or bookstores or a display in a prominent department store window.

PRESS AGENT EXPENSES ($30,000)

Covers costs during the production period both for the press agent's own itemized expenses, such as publications, postage, copying, messengers, long-distance calls, local travel, the reproduction of photos, and other printed materials for press kits, as well as the cost of press-related expenses, such as car service for stars to television or print interviews, make-up and hair styling for the star(s) at these interviews, the production of a "step and repeat" banner repeating the show's title and/or logo for the actors to stand in front of during red carpet interviews, the filming and editing of "B-roll" footage to provide brief excerpts from the show to air alongside television reviews, etc.

PROGRAM ($2,500)

Playbill is the official, free program handed out to patrons in Broadway theaters. This cost covers *Playbill*'s initial charge for setting up the show's "book" or program.

GENERAL AND ADMINISTRATIVE

PRODUCER OFFICE ($12,250)

A weekly expense that commonly begins two weeks prior to the first rehearsal. This sum, representing $1,750/week for seven weeks, is meant to reimburse the producer for his or her general office overhead (rent, assistant, utilities, service contracts on office equipment like a copying machine) and is in addition to itemized reimbursements for such things as copies, messengers, faxes, postage, long-distance telephone calls, etc., which have their own line item further along. The producer office fee may vary depending on how many coproducers there are who feel they play an active, hands-on role in the day-to-day operation of the show and should receive a portion of this fee.

GENERAL MANAGER OFFICE ($8,750)

Similar to the producer's office but for the general manager, at $1,250/ week for seven weeks.

LEGAL ($40,000)

An up-front fee for the attorney to negotiate the option agreement with the author as well as to draft all the financing documents and handle the filings required by the **Securities and Exchange Commission (SEC)**, the NYS attorney general, and the laws of other states where investments are offered. The primary financing documents are (1) the Operating Agreement of the limited liability company (or Limited Partnership Agreement of the limited partnership) formed to produce the play and (2) Subscription Documents (the contract by which investors agree to invest in the company). The production counsel also drafts and negotiates front-money agreements, coproducer agreements, and major investor agreements. The amount of the preproduction legal fee may vary depending on such variables as how many investors are involved, whether all the investors are "accredited" or not, as defined by standards of income and assets established by the SEC (the acceptance of unaccredited investors requires the additional drafting of a Private Placement Memorandum), and the number of states that serve as each investor's legal residence, each state requiring its own filing. Some states have filing fees that must be considered in the budget as well. The production retainer agreement will exclude certain tasks such as immigration, litigation, tax, and music licensing (if there is a significant amount of nonoriginal music to be used in the production).

ACCOUNTING ($11,000)

The fee for theatrical accountants to set up the show and prepare an accounting of production expenses.

PAYROLL TAXES ($34,305)

An estimate of the employer taxes due on salaries paid to company members prior to the first paid public performance. Often, a percentage of 15 percent of salaries is used in this calculation. This figure not only includes the employer's half of federal and state withholding taxes, but it also contains an accrual for quarterly federal and state unemployment taxes as well as quarterly disability insurance premiums.

INSURANCE ($85,000)

A down payment on the premiums for the collective insurance policies a show is both required to carry and elects to carry. These policies will be discussed in detail in chapter 12. The amount of the down payment normally reflects a significant percentage of the total premiums, with the balance being paid off at a negotiated amount per week for a set number of weeks, often not exceeding twenty. Insurance needs vary from show to show; the figure here is an estimate for a Broadway play with fourteen actors, including an elderly star. Because of this fact, I have anticipated the producers electing to take out a special abandonment policy (see page 187), which has a relatively high premium that has to be paid in full up front.

UNION BENEFITS ($60,113)

Union-dictated benefit fund contributions (pension, health, and annuity) for members of theatrical unions such as AEA, ATPAM, SDC, IATSE, USA, Local 764, and Local 798. The general manager should possess all the current union agreements stating their working conditions and the rates for their various salaries, fees, advances, and benefit fund contributions. These rates often increase with each new contract year (versus calendar year) of a union's individual agreement, and the date of a contract year differs from one union/guild/society to another.

VACATION/SICK PAY ($9,441)

An accrual for required vacation and sick pay for AEA members only. Vacation pay is usually estimated at 4 percent of salaries, and sick pay is estimated at 2 percent, but those performers who are paid significantly over scale will have caps on their contribution amounts.

HAULING/SHIPPING ($25,000)

This figure accounts for the trucking of sets, props, lighting equipment, sound equipment, and costumes from their respective shops to the theater. The cost will vary depending on the volume of items to be transported.

TEAMSTERS ($6,000)

In New York City, one cannot unload the trucks referred to in the previous section without employing union teamsters. This sum accounts for their salaries and benefits.

SHOP PREP ($30,000)

This figure accounts for the salaries of personnel required to pull the equipment specified in the lighting and sound plots from the shelves of their respective shops and to prep and label the equipment prior to its being trucked to the theater for load-in. Hopefully, the amount spent on this prep will be more than recouped by having the equipment load-in go more quickly and smoothly at the theater.

TAKE-IN, HANG, AND REHEARSE ($350,000)

Covers those crew salaries needed to install the physical production (sets, props, lights, and sound) and pay for work calls and rehearsal calls prior to the first preview. Once the set, lighting, and sound designs of the show are known, the technical director can do a detailed schedule of crew calls and help the GM zero in on the final number. This line item is one of the most expensive in the production budget and can easily go over budget. It takes a lot of experience to estimate and must be watched very carefully so it does not get out of control. Often one has to hold work notes that are not absolutely essential until enough notes accumulate to justify scheduling a minimum four-hour call.

TELEPHONE, MESSENGER, AND COPYING ($12,000)

An allowance for itemized office reimbursements for these and other expenses, such as postage and overnight couriers, for the producer's and GM's offices.

TRANSPORTATION ($25,000)

Usually airfare, for any company member—most likely to be the author, star(s), or director—who does not live in New York City. Obviously, the class of airfare—economy, business, or first class—an individual agrees to will have a big impact on this line item. The more prominent the players, the less likely it is that they will accept coach airfare—aside from their actual comfort, status concerns preclude them from being seen traveling in any but the top class of airfare offered. On domestic, rather than international, flights, one may be able to find a two-class carrier that will satisfy the individual's airport location and departure time preferences. If one is lucky, the individual may wind up accepting business class travel instead of first class even when first class is contractually stipulated.

HOUSING ($25,000)
A preopening housing allowance for those key creative personnel who do not live locally.

PER DIEM ($18,900)
Covers a food allowance for any out-of-town members, again most likely to be the author, director, or star(s). Although the amount specified contractually is called a per diem (per day), it is paid out weekly, often in cash.

CAR SERVICE ($15,000)
Stars expect the show to provide them with car service for show-related activities. They can't be expected to walk to the corner and hail a cab; they're stars, they'd be mobbed! Sometimes one can delay the start of the car service until the actor begins working at the theater. Although one can negotiate the base cost of the pick-ups to and from the actor's hotel or apartment and the theater with the car service, unanticipated waiting time or extra stops greatly increases the base cost. This figure is a calculation for two people, with a round trip within Manhattan six times a week for five weeks, with a car service of the show's selection. Often the negotiation for a car service includes a preapproved, but nontransferable, specified number of hours of waiting time per week.

SECURITY ($3,000)
A major star will frequently require that the show hire special security to provide him or herself with safe entrance to and exit from the theater. This sum represents one week (tech week) of such service.

OPENING NIGHT ($50,000)
Covers the cost of a party and company gift. Of course the size of the theater/number of guests invited plus how elaborate the food and décor is

will affect this figure. This sum is intended to cover the cost of a party for five hundred to six hundred people and provides for a hot buffet dinner, a limited bar, and a modest company gift.

INTERIM HOUSING ($12,600)
Experience has shown it is wise not to rent an apartment for a star until she or her authorized representative has seen it in person and given her assurance that it is acceptable. Thus, sometimes it is wise to allocate some initial hotel time for a star when she first arrives in town. This sum represents an allowance for four people at $450/night for one week.

REAL ESTATE BROKER FEES ($20,000)
If one expects to rent apartments for stars, one will undoubtedly have to pay a broker's fee to the broker who finds the apartment. This sum represents two fees of $10,000 each.

MISCELLANEOUS ($10,257)
A catch-all category for things like producer entertaining; also, used to "sweeten" the preceding figures, so that the production expense figure is a nice round number.

DEVELOPMENTAL COSTS ($16,500)
This category may or may not be needed, but often a producer has to personally front certain legitimate production costs, such as a developmental reading or workshop of the play, before the legal entity has been formed to produce the play. In this event, the producer is entitled to be reimbursed for these provable expenses once the entity has been formed.

TOTAL ESTIMATED PRODUCTION EXPENSE ($2,760,000)
The sum of all the figures above, representing the amount of money anticipated to be actually spent by the time one gets to the first paid public performance or preview. After this point in time, operating begins. This production expense figure is what recoupment is based on, since, from an

accounting point of view, the budget figures below this line are considered to be assets and recoverable, not expenses. Thus, recoupment is actually based on a lower figure than the amount of the show's total capitalization. Remember this fact; more about it later.

ADVANCES, BONDS, AND DEPOSITS

Author ($40,000)

This is where the author's option payment is accounted for, as long as all of it can be considered an advance against royalties, plus the author's royalty advance. This advance may be lower for a revival than it is for a new play, particularly if the piece is no longer a hot property that is much in demand.

Director ($25,000)

Accounts for a contractual royalty advance. SDC requires that part of the director's initial compensation be treated as an advance against royalty payments, and only allows those payments to the director in excess of a contractual minimum guarantee to reduce the amount of the advance each week. As in the fee, this is an above minimum amount for an in-demand director.

Scenic Designer ($2,917)

The current USA minimum for this particular category (at the time of writing).

Costume Designer ($2,394)

The current USA minimum for this particular category (at the time of writing).

Lighting Designer ($2,188)

The current USA minimum for this particular category (at the time of writing).

Sound Designer ($0)

No advance was required in this particular negotiation.

AEA ($188,312)

Equity requires a bond for their members consisting of two weeks contractual salary (not necessarily the same as rehearsal salary), plus two weeks of Media Payment, per diem (if applicable), pension, health and annuity contributions, and a bookkeeping fee. There are caps on the amount of over-scale salary and per diem that are pensionable.

NOTE: Equity's requirement that the producer place a bond with them for two week's contractual salary, plus benefits, for all cast and stage managers arose in response to abuses by irresponsible producers, especially in the days when it was common for shows to tour out of town prior to coming into Broadway. The musical *On the Twentieth Century* starts with the megalomaniacal theatrical producer Oscar Jaffe suffering a disastrous flop out of town and fleeing in the middle of the night, leaving the actors stranded in Chicago without pay or providing them with any means of transportation back to New York.

ATPAM ($18,401)

ATPAM requires a similar bond on behalf of the company manager and press agent. House managers are on the theater payroll, not the show payroll.

THEATER ($0)

This is a contract negotiation point and often is affected by how well the theater owner knows, and has confidence in, the lead producer.

HOUSING DEPOSITS ($20,000)

Needed if apartments will be rented. This sum represents two deposits for rentals of $10,000/month each.

IATSE BOND ($5,000)

Represents a bond for two Pink IATSE stagehands at a flat $2,500 for each.

RESERVE ($435,789)

A cushion, or sinking fund, to help subsidize operating losses in weeks in which the box office revenue is less than the show's expenses. This represents more than one full week of operating expenses. A reserve is essential to protect the larger production costs and can help a show buy time and "get on its feet" during the first few weeks of operation. The hope is always to presell the show well enough so that previews will not reduce the reserve, and a sizable war chest will still be available as of opening night. Remember, too, that any cost overruns in production will reduce the reserve.

NOTE: Sometimes a producer has difficulty raising their full target capitalization and elects to form the producing entity based on the alternative minimum capitalization amount specified in its papers. This invariably reduces the amount of the budgeted reserve and is a potentially dangerous move. I've had producers say to me "Don't worry. I have deep pockets. If we slash the reserve now, I can always make a priority loan to the company later if needed." If the show gets terrible reviews across the boards, it will probably close, and this may not be an issue. If, however, the show winds up getting mixed reviews—some good, some bad—the decision to reduce the capitalization can prove fatal. If money has been budgeted for a reserve, it is readily available to pay for additional advertising and marketing that can fight mixed reviews and possibly turn the show around. If, however, the producer has initially reduced the amount of the reserve and it is now fully depleted, he might suddenly lose his confidence in making a priority loan and reconsider, worrying that doing so might be throwing good money after bad.

TOTAL CAPITALIZATION ($3,500,000)

This is the sum of the production costs, advances/bonds/deposits, and reserve. It represents the full capitalization needed to produce the show, although only the production costs need to be recouped before the show is officially in net profit. The production costs will be placed in a more meaningful context when the operating budget has been calculated, revealing the operating expenses, breakeven figure, and various recoupment scenarios. These will all be examined in the following chapter.

		A BROADWAY PLAY (Preliminary & Tenative—for Discussion Purposes Only)	CAP: 3,500,000
A Broadway Theater 1050 Seats			1st Draft: 11/18/16

PHYSICAL PRODUCTION

Scenery	$425,000	
Automation	25,000	
Props/Dressing	25,000	
Rehearsal Props/Scenery	7,500	
Dressing Room Costs	7,500	
Costumes	40,000	
Hair/Make-Up	9,000	for 2 female leads
Electrics	16,500	
Carpentry/Electrics/Sound (Perishables)	15,000	
Sound (Preparation)	7,500	
Sound (Recording)	10,000	
	Subtotal: 588,000	

FEES

Author (Option Payment)	0	accounted for as advance
Director	50,000	above scale for prominent director
Executive Producer	35,000	
General Manager	32,500	
Scenic Designer	13,217	minimum, multi set
Costume Designer	9,920	minimum, 8-15 characters, plus period
Lighting Designer	9,915	minimum, multi set
Sound Designer	7,500	how much new work?
Wig Designer	5,000	
Composer	7,500	
Tech Supervisor	18,000	modest
Press Preproduction	7,500	
Marketing Consultant	7,500	
Casting Director	18,000	based on comparable recent show
Dialect Coach	5,000	
Make-up Consultant	3,000	
Assistant Scenic Designer	(1,494 x 6)	8,964	
Assistant Costume Designer	(1,494 x 6)	8,964	
Assistant Lighting Designer	(1,494 x 6)	8,964	
Assistant Sound Designer	(1,494 x 5)	7,470	
Assistant Director	(750 x 10)	7,500	
Prop Shopper	15,000	
Production Assistant	9,000	
	Subtotal: 295,414	

REHEARSAL/TECH SALARIES (4 Wk Reh, 1 Wk Tech)

Stars	(4 x 2,013 x 5)	40,270	includes Media Payment
Principals	(4 x 2,013 x 5)	40,270	
Understudies	(4 x 2,013 x 5)	40,270	start as of 3rd week ?
Stage Managers	(1 x 2,977 x 7.17, 1 x 2,318 x 6.17)	36,537	
Producers	(1 x 3,750 x 7)	26,250	
General Manager	(1 x 3,250 x 7)	22,750	
Company Manager	(1 x 2,346 x 7.17)	16,821	
Press Agent	(1 x 2,513 x 5)	12,565	
Wardrobe	(1 x 1,919 x 3, 2 x 1,648 x 3)	15,644	2 dressers enough?
Hair/Make-up	(1 x 1,464 x 3)	4,393	needed?
Pink Crew	(2 x 2,200 x 3)	13,200	how many?
		Subtotal: 268,970	

REHEARSAL/PREVIEW EXPENSES

Theater Expenses	105,000	
Halls (Audition/Rehearsal)	14,000	
Stage Manager & Departmental	6,000	
	Subtotal: 125,000	

ADVERTISING & PUBLICITY

Print/Media	150,000
Outdoor	57,500
Direct Response	130,000

Production/Printing		105,000	
Front of House		20,000	
Miscellaneous		15,000	
Radio		35,000	
Website Services		22,500	
Marketing		35,000	
Press Agent Expenses		30,000	
Program		2,500	
		Subtotal: 602,500	

GENERAL & ADMINISTRATIVE

Producer Office	(1750 x 7)	12,250	2 weeks prior
General Manager Office	(1250 x 7)	8,750	2 weeks prior
Legal		40,000	
Accounting		11,000	
Payroll Taxes		34,305	
Insurance		85,000	includes D+O & Business Interruption
Union Benefits		60,113	
Vacation/Sick		9,441	
Hauling/Shipping		25,000	
Teamsters		6,000	
Shop Prep		30,000	
Take-in, Hang & Rehearse		350,000	
Telephone, Messenger & Copying		12,000	
Transportation		25,000	needed ???
Housing		25,000	needed ???
Per Diem		18,900	Director plus 2 stars
Car Service		15,000	2 stars, from 1st rehearsal
Security		3,000	just tech week?
Opening Night		50,000	
Interim Housing		12,600	1 week in hotel for 4?
Real Estate Broker Fees		20,000	estimate for 2 apartments
Miscellaneous		10,257	
		Subtotal: 863,616	

DEVELOPMENTAL COSTS		*Subtotal: 16,500*	guesstimate

TOTAL ESTIMATED PRODUCTION EXPENSE   2,760,00

ADVANCES, BONDS, AND DEPOSITS

Author	(Advance)	40,000	as per our current proposal on table
Director	(Advance)	25,000	negotiated
Scenic Designer	(Advance)	2,917	minimum, multi set
Costume Designer	(Advance)	2,394	minimum, 8–15 characters, plus period
Lighting Designer	(Advance)	2,188	minimum, multi-set
Sound Designer	(Advance)	0	
AEA		188,312	based on est. performance salaries
ATPAM		18,401	
Theater Deposit		0	
Housing Deposits		20,000	for 2 apartments
IATSE Bond		5,000	2 people?
		Subtotal: 304,211	

RESERVE		*Subtotal: 435,789*	

3

The Operating Budget

Now that we know how much it will cost to produce the show and get it to the first paid public performance (**preview**), we need to understand its weekly operating expenses. The operating budget at the end of this chapter reveals the show's estimated **fixed weekly expenses**, its estimated **variable expenses** (those dependent on the fluctuating box office gross, i.e., ticket sales), its weekly **nut**, or **breakeven** (the minimum gross needed to exactly cover all the show's expenses, leaving zero profit or loss), the maximum **capacity gross** (100 percent of full price ticket sales), and what percentage of capacity gross the show's breakeven represents. It also offers several different **recoupment scenarios** that show how many weeks it will take to recoup the show's **production costs**, based on the size of the theater and a specified average ticket price, at several different percentages of capacity—for example, sixteen weeks to recoup at 70 percent of capacity, twelve weeks to recoup at 80 percent of capacity, etc.

SALARIES
Stars ($64,500)
This figure represents the contractual, rather than the union minimum, salaries for an estimated four stars, which begin as of the first paid public performance. This supposes three stars at an average weekly guarantee of

$20,000 each (remember, often the earliest budget drafts are done before a star has been identified, and almost certainly before the star's salary has been negotiated), and a fourth at $4,500 a week. Notice I say "guarantee," as stars often additionally receive a percentage of the gross. Unless the initial preview performance occurs on the first performance day of a work week (i.e., a Monday or Tuesday), the week in which the first preview occurs is often a split week, meaning a performer's salary is split between being prorated one-seventh of his or her minimum for any rehearsal days worked during the final week leading up to performances and one-eighth of the negotiated contractual salary for any performances given. If a star's salary is over scale (i.e., above minimum or scale), the contract should be written such that the over-scale portion of the star's salary includes payment for any items that would otherwise be considered additional expenses, as outlined in the following paragraph. Otherwise, those additional expenses would trigger further compensation on top of the over-scale salary! A sample star contract will be reviewed at greater length in chapter 5.

PRINCIPALS ($9,200)

This figure anticipates four modest speaking roles at an average of $2,300/ week, each of whom also understudies one of the star roles, requiring additional payment. At the time of writing, the current Equity minimum plus the Media Payment comes to $2,013.49/week, a **term increment** (required when you contract an actor for a set amount of time, say six months, and do not allow the actor the option of giving notice and leaving before then) is $206/week, and one understudy assignment for a performing actor is $53/week, totaling $2,272.49. Equity also dictates specific weekly premiums for a variety of additional duties, such as dance captain ($383.40), fight captain ($75), extraordinary risk ($20), partial swing ($15), and scenic or prop moves not within the scope of the actor's character or coinciding with the actor's entrance into or exit from a scene ($8). Budgeting even a small amount (in this case, another $27.51) above the exact amount you are required to pay has both psychological and practical value. Telling someone his salary is $2,300/week sounds a lot better than telling him it is $2,272.49! The higher figure also allows the actor's agent to tell his client that he negotiated a (slightly!) better than minimum deal, which can be a point of pride for a performer. At the same time, if it is so stated in the contract, any amount above minimum can be applied toward payment of any of the additional duty premiums, should they be assigned after the contract has been signed (say during the course of rehearsal). If, in the end, the sum of an actor's assigned additional duties winds up exceeding the amount above minimum indicated in his or her initial contract, then a rider to the contract stating the new, higher, contractual salary has to be executed and filed with the union.

UNDERSTUDIES ($9,000)

A similar calculation to the one for principals, minus the increment a performing principal receives for understudying another role or roles. This sum covers four people budgeted at current (time of writing) minimum, plus a Media Payment, a term increment, and a modest amount above their total to "sweeten" that figure, which can also double as payment for a few minor additional duties that may or may not be assigned.

NOTE: Some people feel it is extravagant to pay understudies a term increment, but because they are covering lead roles, and the director, who may not subsequently be available, has already approved them, I feel it is wise to pay a little extra to hold onto them. It can be costly to replace understudies. There will be additional casting costs, audition costs, rehearsal costs, costuming costs, publicity costs (front-of-house photos will almost certainly need to be reshot), crew costs (for a put-in rehearsal), etc. Finally, if an understudy is really good in a role, why wouldn't one want to hold on to that person as a valuable member of the company and preclude his or her option of leaving?

STAGE MANAGERS ($5,296)

Accounts for a veteran production stage manager (PSM) at $150/week above minimum and an assistant stage manager (ASM) at minimum, both receiving a Media Payment as well. A term increment is rarely budgeted for the ASM, as this position is far easier to replace than that of the PSM. In this instance, the PSM is budgeted at $150 above minimum but does not receive a term increment as well. If the PSM has a long-standing relationship with the producer or director, it is highly unlikely he or she would ever hand in a two-week notice, leaving the company (not to mention the producer and director) feeling abandoned.

PRODUCERS ($3,750)
A weekly producer fee, as distinct from a royalty or office charge. This sum may be divided between several lead producers.

GENERAL MANAGER ($3,250)
This figure represents the current market rate for an experienced GM to manage a play on Broadway. It is separate from an office fee.

COMPANY MANAGER ($2,346)
Represents a weekly salary at $100/week above the current, at time of writing, ATPAM company manager minimum and includes 8.5 percent vacation pay.

PRESS AGENT ($2,513)
As with the company manager, this figure represents a weekly salary at $100/week above the current ATPAM press agent minimum at time of writing, and includes 8.5 percent vacation pay.

WARDROBE ($5,632)
Allows for a supervisor and two dressers. The supervisor's compensation includes an extra $100/week fee for his or her kit rental—iron, ironing board, steamer, threads and buttons, etc. The two dressers are budgeted at minimum, with a projected additional total of eight hours of day work for both, each week.

HAIR AND MAKE-UP ($1,464)
Provides for one person, although in the end two might be needed.

PINK CREW ($4,400)
Two people at the going market rate of $2,200 each, projected as needed for the positions of sound board operator and props.

DEPARTMENTAL EXPENSE

This section consists primarily of weekly accruals in various departments, that is, sums of money to be accounted for on a weekly profit and loss accounting statement, which may not actually be charged to the show on a weekly basis but may be submitted monthly. Accruals should be reviewed with the accountant about once every four weeks to check if they need to be adjusted, either up or down, in relation to the actual expenses.

STAGE MANAGER ($200)
To be put against receipts for things like first-aid supplies, coffee and tea paraphernalia, office supplies, batteries, cups, company birthday cakes, doorman tips, etc.

CARPENTRY ($650)
An allowance for set-related repairs.

PROPS/PERISHABLES ($150)
This category will largely depend on the requirements of the play. Are there perishables (food, drinks, cigarettes) that are consumed on stage nightly and need to be constantly replenished? Are newspapers or letters used, which have a limited stage life? Does the action of the play call for a fight, where an item is broken every performance—a vase, or a glass unicorn? All these factors will affect this department's budget.

ELECTRIC/SOUND ($150)
Serves as an accrual against periodic bills for items like new colored gel, replacement bulbs, wireless microphone batteries, or other departmental expenses.

NOTE: It is a little known fact outside of the theater community that in shows using wireless microphones, the sound department typically includes condoms among its reimbursable expenses. Why, you well may ask? The condoms (nonlubricated only, no need for special colors or textures) are used to wrap the transmitter portion of a wireless microphone's body pack and serve to protect the transmitter from body sweat. One condom per transmitter per performance is the rule, so if you have a musical with a large cast, you'll probably need to buy in bulk!

PRESS AGENT ($300)
A weekly accrual that goes against monthly itemized bills from the press office to cover the costs of such expenses as copying, messengers, faxing, publications, postage, taxis, and long-distance telephone calls.

REHEARSAL/WORK CALL EXPENSE ($500)
An accrual to pay for crew calls, with any members of the carpentry, electrics (including sound), and/or props departments that may be needed to run a rehearsal or staff a work call for repairs or routine maintenance. Normally, the theater is available for rehearsal without additional rent if appropriate advance notice is given. Rehearsals are often done with work lights and may not require an electrician to operate the show's lights. Depending on how many scene changes there are or how much prop dressing is needed to set up different scenes, crew may need to be brought in to give the rehearsing actors a real sense of what they will encounter on stage or experience during a scene change.

WARDROBE/COSTUME REPLACEMENT/CLEANING ($250)
An accrual to account for departmental expenses like laundry detergent, spray starch, a new ironing board cover, sewing supplies, shoe polish or dye, as well as weekly dry-cleaning. One might also need an accrual toward the cost of costume replacement if the show is expected to have a long run or if it is likely there will be cast changes. The number of costumes in the show, whether they need to be sent out for dry-cleaning (rather than machine washed by the wardrobe department in the theater), and if so, how often, will affect the cost of this line item.

RENTALS
ELECTRICS ($2,500)
Covers the weekly rental to the electrics shop for the lighting package. This sum is a "typical" current rate for a lighting package suitable for a play. It does not account for moving lights, like Vari-Lites, which tend to

be more expensive to rent (as well as to program). The weekly rate may be negotiated to decrease over time, for example, the first twelve weeks at one rate, a lower rate thereafter. Most shops often scramble to meet their own weekly payroll, so if you are confident your show will be around for awhile, you can try offering a large up-front payment toward your rental. This sum should cover a set period of time but, in exchange for paying it in advance, should reflect a *lower* weekly amount than the sum you had initially agreed to.

SOUND ($2,500)
Represents the analogous sum paid to the sound shop for all sound equipment rented. This sum does not cover wireless microphones for the company—often used in a musical but rarely in a play, where foot mics frequently suffice to reinforce sound instead.

AUTOMATION ($3,000)
Will only be needed if required by the scenic design.

MISCELLANEOUS ($500)
A catch-all category for items like a genie lift to reach lights on the grid during work calls or for trusses (frameworks) that are rented to hang lights from.

FIXED ROYALTIES
As opposed to percentage royalties calculated on varying gross receipts or net profits, fixed royalties are set, unfluctuating amounts paid to various personnel for their on-going contribution to the show. Sometimes these set amounts will rise at specific, higher thresholds of the gross weekly box office receipts (**GWBOR**). As a GM, you should always strive to protect the show by keeping expenses down when it has little or no profit to prevent the show from losing money. When the show is grossing well above its breakeven point and making a lot of profit, there is room to be generous.

AUTHOR/DIRECTOR/PRODUCER ($0)
These key creatives are primarily receiving a variable (percentage) royalty, accounted for in the following recoupment scenarios, either based on the show's box office gross or on net profits, which is why nothing is

accounted for here. In point of fact, even these royalties have a **minimum weekly guarantee** (**MWG**) that must be paid every week, even in losing, breakeven, or **Grey Zone** weeks (when the gross is only ten percent above breakeven or less). In this budget, these MWGs are accounted for later on in the recoupment scenarios, under the breakeven column.

SET DESIGNER ($500)

The fixed designer royalty amounts on this show are designed to be negotiated in tiers, based on rising GWBOR. Five hundred dollars is the minimum amount, good for grosses up to $400,000. This is higher than the stipulated United Scenic Artists (USA) suggested minimum but is still a very modest sum for Broadway. There are bumps in payment beyond the minimum of $500: if the GWBOR are $400,001to $500,000, the designer receives an additional $150, or $650 total; if $500,001 to $650,000, he or she receives an additional $300, or $800 total; if $650,001 to $800,000, an additional $500, or $1,000 total; and if $800,001 or more, an additional $750, or $1,250 total. These bumps are reflected in the budget's recoupment charts at different GWBOR points.

COSTUME DESIGNER ($500)

Analogous to set designer.

LIGHTING DESIGNER ($500)

Analogous to set designer.

SOUND DESIGNER ($500)

Analogous to set designer.

COMPOSER ($500)

This can sometimes be the same person as the sound designer, with the same agent representing him or her in both capacities, so it is wise to budget the same royalty for both contributions.

CASTING ($750)

This sum may depend on the size of the cast. Sometimes this sum will have a prenegotiated increase beginning post recoupment (the week after recoupment of production expenses).

FIGHT DIRECTOR ($100)
A very modest sum, budgeted in this instance because the script indicates some fairly minimal physical activity—a single punch, or an actor falling down—which may require the brief involvement of a fight director to safely choreograph the action.

TECH SUPERVISOR ($750)
It is standard for a technical supervisor to receive a fixed weekly royalty on a show as compensation for his or her ongoing availability to deal with any problems or repairs to the physical production that may arise.

MUSIC RIGHTS ($450)
Even though original music has been composed for the play to cover transitions, sometimes snatches of copyrighted songs are heard (on a television or radio, for example) or sung by a character within a given scene. If the sound design (or script) indicates specific music, it is necessary to approach the company that has the publishing rights to the music and legally obtain permission for its use. Although these companies may not be accustomed to licensing their properties for use in the theater, it is often possible to negotiate a modest fixed weekly royalty for the music's use, especially if favored nations (the same terms for everyone) is invoked. This figure is based on three such songs/compositions, at $150/week each, proratable based on an eight-performance week. Obtaining music rights can be a long, arduous process—first in finding the correct publishing company who currently owns the material, then in getting someone to respond to your query. Often one has to send a detailed letter to the appropriate source telling them about the project, giving them the exact timing of each excerpt requested, and enclosing the script pages that contain the scene in which the music will be played.

ADVERTISING AND PUBLICITY
This section allots a general amount of money to be used for advertising and promoting the play, conventionally budgeted to be between 20 and 25 percent of the total operating budget. Part of it is an accrual (to account for bills that have not been received yet but are anticipated), and part is an amortization (for larger sums that have already been spent but whose expense will be distributed over multiple weeks).

AVERAGE ADVERTISING WEEKLY TOTAL ($50,000)

This represents the total average weekly sum the advertising agency has to spend—on print ads, ABC directory listings, direct response (email blasts or a direct mail offer), digital ads on websites, radio ads, television ads, outdoor advertising (billboards, commuter rail line station platforms, telephone kiosks, bus sides), as well as the studio production costs needed to design these items. Print ads are normally priced by the width of the ad (measured in number of columns), multiplied by the height of the ad (measured in inches), times a per-column rate per inch. For example, a "2 by 2" (two columns wide, two inches tall) ad running on a day where the per-column inch cost is $525 would cost 2 x 2 x $525, or $2,100). ABC's are usually priced according to a per-line cost, with a minimum requirement of ten lines. Obviously, the budget does not allow one to do everything every week, so the ad agency varies the initiatives—some weeks have radio in them, others television, some weeks you run a bigger print ad, other weeks you send out a direct mail piece, etc.

Some outdoor advertising is seasonal—preferable in dry, warm weather when people are more inclined to linger outdoors than in cold, wet months.

AMORTIZATION FOR ADDITIONAL MEDIA/MAILINGS ($5,000)

Periodically, one will want to do a special campaign push—a new direct mailing, a flight of radio ads—which exceeds the regular weekly advertising budget. This figure allows one to write off an extraordinary expense over several weeks.

MARKETING FEES ($5,500)

More and more, advertising agencies are trying to bring the marketing in-house, so the agency can control and coordinate both endeavors (and budgets). Sometimes, philosophically, a producer will not want this, feeling there is something to be gained by bringing a variety of people to the table, each offering his or her own area of expertise. This sum accounts for various fees or commissions that certain marketing individuals or firms may charge.

MARKETING BUDGET ($2,500)

An allocation to pay for the cost of specific marketing endeavors themselves—the expenses involved in having a booth advertising the show at an appropriate trade convention, for example—as distinct from the marketing fees discussed in the previous section, to the individuals or companies providing the service.

OTHER ($2,000)
A catch-all category for various miscellaneous items, like paying someone to distribute flyers for the show at TKTS, the same-day discount ticket booth whose flagship location is at 47th Street and Broadway.

THEATER EXPENSE
Typically, a Broadway theater suited for a play, rather than a musical, has approximately 1,000 seats and generates expenses, prior to the theater owner receiving a percentage of the box office gross, of around $90,000 a week. The actual costs vary from theater to theater, and the way this sum is broken down may differ between theater owners (the majority of Broadway theaters are operated by only three organizations—the Shubert Organization, the Nederlander Organization, and Jujamcyn Theaters), but this sum is a pretty reliable base figure at the time of writing. In this example, the expenses are allocated as follows.

RENT GUARANTEE/HOUSE SHARE ($15,000)
The rental guarantee, stated in the theater lease, is often against a percentage of the gross, currently at a standard of 6 percent for plays. Thus the guarantee of $15,000 against 6 percent covers all rental owed up to GWBOR of $250,000. Thereafter, the show pays an additional 6 percent, which is accounted for in the section of the recoupment chart that includes variable expenses.

FIXED OPERATING CHARGE ($15,000)
A flat fee, without detail.

STAGEHANDS (3) ($15,000)
This accounts for the minimum of three house heads (in carpentry, electrics, and props), plus vacation, 19 percent payroll taxes, and union benefits. There may be additional premiums if you plan on having a Sunday performance or if house heads are getting a weekly fee for taking the place of Pink production stagehands. The number of stagehands needed to run the show will vary according to the technical needs of the play.

Other Staff ($27,000)

Accounts for the salaries, payroll taxes, and benefits for all union theater personnel other than stagehands: treasurers, house manager, ticket takers, ushers, porters, stage doormen, engineers, cleaning people, etc. In a Broadway theater, every single position is unionized, even the porter who sweeps up cigarette butts from the sidewalk in front of the theater.

House Expenses ($18,000)

Covers expenses such as utilities, insurance, cartage, pest control, remote telephone sales service, armored car transport (to transport box office revenue to the bank), credit card terminals, bottled water, toilet paper, etc.

GENERAL AND ADMINISTRATIVE

Producer's Office Fee ($1,750)

The same weekly figure as in the production budget (see page 43) now carried forward into operating weeks.

General Manager Office Fee ($1,250)

The same weekly figure as in the production budget (see page 43) now carried forward into operating weeks.

Legal ($750)

A weekly retainer negotiated in advance with the show attorney as compensation for routine show maintenance activities. The retainer normally begins the week of the first paid public performance and is proratable.

Accounting ($1,000)

This amount is prenegotiated with the show's accountant and includes payment for preparing the weekly profit and loss statement. This amount is fairly typical for a Broadway play at the time of writing.

Insurance ($2,000)

When taken together with the up-front down payment in the production budget (see page 43), this amount will, in a set number of weeks to be determined with the insurance broker, pay off the full cost of all the show's insurance premiums. Insurance needs will vary from show to show. This amount accounts for all the basic premiums a play requires as well as two elected policies: (1) business interruption and (2) directors and officers. The former can be quite expensive and will be explained further in chapter 12.

Payroll Taxes ($7,028)

This figure will obviously vary depending on the amount of your salaried payroll. A calculation using 15 percent of salaries is used here and excludes anyone being paid a fee versus a salary.

Union Benefits ($9,622)

A weekly figure corresponding to the sum of all the required union benefits referred to in the production budget (see page 43).

Vacation/Sick Pay ($4,962)

An accrual of 6 percent of all Equity salaries. On Broadway, Equity members are entitled to 4 percent vacation pay (capped at the minimum for a stage manager of a musical), which accrues from the first day of employment and is payable regardless of the length of employment. Sick pay is also accrued based on an estimate of 2 percent of actor's salary. The sum of the two represents the 6 percent figure used.

In actuality, the payout of sick pay is more complicated than it might appear—sick pay is meant to compensate and primarily benefit actors being paid on the low end of salaries, and its benefits decrease as an actor's contractual salary rises. Thus an actor being paid no more than $150 above the current stage manager's (musical) current minimum (exclusive of Media Payment or per diem) earns one sick day credit for each four weeks of employment if the show was organized for more than three months or was a limited engagement announced for less than three months. If the actor is sick and has an unused sick day credit that can be applied, his or her salary is not docked one-eighth for a missed performance. When the show closes, an actor in this category may be paid for up to eleven unused sick day credits, but based on one-eighth of the minimum of his or her applicable Equity salary category, not the contractual salary. In the Equity rulebook, "actor" is a generic term that can also apply to stage managers and assistant stage managers, each of whom has an individual, stipulated minimum salary.

Actors earning more than $150 above the current stage manager's (musical) current minimum (exclusive of Media Payment or per diem) but not more than $3,250, earn one sick day credit for each four weeks of employment, capped at one-eighth of the current stage manager's (musical) current minimum, and are not entitled to be paid for any unused sick day credits when the show closes. Actors earning between $3,250 and $4,250 receive even less sick pay benefits, and actors earning in excess of $4,250 receive none.

Per Diems ($2,100)
An allocation for two stars, each receiving a per diem of $150, or $1,050 per week. This is intended for food only and is separate from any housing allowance or negotiated apartment or hotel accommodations, accounted for in the following line item.

Housing ($5,000)
An estimate for two stars, based on $10,000/month, $2,500/week, for each. It could be for an apartment or a hotel. If you can persuade the actor to take a hotel, it is preferable, as there will not be a deposit, broker's fee, or the extensive paperwork that an apartment lease or sublet usually entails.

Car Service ($3,000)
For two stars, based on an average cost of $1,500/week each. This figure represents a modest base cost if you can cut a deal with a car service for a sedan, not a limousine, for two round trips a day within Manhattan, six days a week. (Actors rarely choose to go home between shows on matinee days.) It accounts for waiting time of eight hours a week but does not account for more waiting time, extra stops, or if the star lives outside of Manhattan (for example, in Westchester or Connecticut).

Security ($3,000)
Accounts for the services of an experienced security guard, who will escort your stars between their car and the stage door when they arrive at or depart from the theater.

Closing Costs ($9,000)
An accrual to help account for the costs involved in closing a show—stagehand labor to strike the sets, lights, sound, and props, trucking, dumpsters,

close-out salaries for the general manager and company manager, final accounting costs, return star airfares, etc. The load-out costs for the physical production are the single biggest component here, and the show's technical supervisor can help estimate this expense once he or she has calculated the take-in costs.

MISCELLANEOUS ($2,937)
A modest catch-all category for items like payroll processing fees or producer personal expense reimbursements. This category is also used to "sweeten" all the proceeding figures in the operating budget and create a total estimated fixed expense figure that is a nice, round figure.

Based on all the proceeding numbers, the total estimated fixed weekly expense to operate this show is $335,000. Unless one subsequently negotiates cuts or waivers in any area, this is the expected amount of your fixed, as distinct from variable, expenses. This figure does not equal the full amount of one's breakeven, or nut, but comprises the major component of it.

At the end of the attached operating budget is a recoupment chart (see page 67), listing the additional variable expenses (dependent on the fluctuating gross or net) and showing six different gross scenarios that reveal how long recoupment (of production expenses) would take in each instance.

Based on an average ticket price of $109 (identified in the upper left corner of the chart), in a theater of 1,050 seats with eight performances a week, at 100 percent of capacity, the theoretical weekly capacity gross would be $915,600, which does not include any seats sold at a premium rate or at a discount, only at regular box office prices. To the right of this 100 percent capacity column are five other scenarios, at 90, 80, 70, 50, and 38 percent of that capacity. Let's start with the column to the farthest right, which shows the financial situation at a gross of $347,873, representing 38 percent of capacity.

This column reveals the show's nut, or breakeven, the gross necessary to just cover all the show's expenses, yielding neither profit nor loss. (See how at the bottom of the column there is a zero in the line labeled Profit/Loss.) A good rule of thumb is that breakeven should occur at 50 percent of capacity or less.

NOTE: "How did the show's nut come to be called that?" I hear you ask. Well, I'll tell you. Long ago, when actors belonged to roving troupes that went from town to town plying their trade, they and their gear traveled in horse-drawn carts. When the troupe first arrived in town, the local authorities, who clearly had been burned before, removed the nut from the axel of their carts, preventing the troupe from sneaking out of town before all of their financial obligations had been met. When the authorities were convinced the troupe had paid all that they owed, the company was said to have "made their nut" and it was returned to them.

It has already been established that the fixed expenses are $335,000. Inevitably there are additional percentage, or variable, expenses that also have to be accounted for. In this example, it is estimated that each of three stars will receive a guarantee of $20,000 (contained within the fixed expenses) plus 5 percent of any gross above $375,000. At this gross point of $347,873, no additional royalty has yet been earned. The designers' minimums are good up to $400,000, so like the stars, no additional compensation is due at this gross. The theater, however, receives a guarantee of $15,000 against 6 percent of the gross, which covers their compensation up to a gross of $250,000. Thus, even at breakeven, the theater will be due an additional 6 percent of any gross above $250,000, in this instance equal to 6 percent of $97,873, or $5,872. The creative team—author, director, and producer (and licensor if the show has had a previous production at another theater that has negotiated future royalty participation for itself)—although normally paid a percentage of the gross, usually only receives a negotiated minimum weekly guarantee (MWG) in losing weeks, breakeven weeks, or weeks where the gross does not exceed 110 percent of breakeven (called the Grey Zone). Those negotiated MWGs are indicated in this column. The breakdown of the percentage royalty package is indicated in the column to the left of the 100 percent capacity column, and in this example, the total royalty package equals 10 percent, of which the author is earning 5 percent, or half.

Notice that with fixed expenses of $335,000, one actually has to gross $347,873 to cover both the fixed and variable expenses. Since there is neither profit nor loss at breakeven, the show will never pay back one cent to its investors from weekly operating profit at this level. And yet, theoretically, the show could run forever, since it is paying all its expenses. And by continuing to operate, the show may participate in a variety of other, valuable, subsidiary income streams that can help the investors to recoup—merchandise sales (scripts, CDs, T-shirts, mugs, refrigerator magnets, etc.), stock and amateur licensing (to regional theaters, community theaters, high schools, and summer camps), a television or film sale, first- and second-class touring productions, licensed sit-down productions in other major US cities, foreign productions (such as in London), etc.—as long as the rights to participate in those areas have been negotiated for in the author's option agreement.

NOTE: I have a GM friend and colleague who managed a very successful Off Broadway show that ran for close to ten years. He confided to me that Off Broadway, the show normally operated close to breakeven, rarely making any significant weekly profit or loss. However, because of its ability to keep running, serve as a flagship production for the property, and, most importantly, create the perception of the show being a long-running, smash hit, the show eventually became a worldwide phenomenon, was translated into twenty-six foreign languages, and generated more than 8,000 productions worldwide! The subsidiary income streams that the property generated and shared, in part, with the original Off Broadway partnership and its investors enabled everyone involved to make a very nice profit indeed. But the key to all of this was keeping the running costs of the original Off Broadway production low enough so that the show could break even and stay open, year in and year out, even in the traditional doldrums of the year (September, with back-to-school concerns and major Jewish holidays, or January and February, with post-holiday exhaustion, lousy weather, and overextended finances).

In the next column to the left of Breakeven, things have started to change. At 50 percent of capacity, a gross of $457,800, the total expenses leave a weekly operating profit of $50,632. Star overages (additional percentage compensation beyond their guarantees), designer royalty bumps, and full creative percentage royalties have all kicked in. At this level of operation, it would take more than fifty-four weeks to recoup production costs.

At 70 percent of capacity, things have improved markedly. The weekly profit now totals $176,985. At this rate, one could recoup production costs in under sixteen weeks.

NOTE: With an average ticket price of $109, in a theater of 1,050 seats, at 70 percent of capacity, the show could recoup in just under sixteen weeks. The chart shows capacity to be $915,600 ($109 x 1050 seats x 8 performances), and 70 percent of that figure represents a gross of $640,920. But remember, mathematically, 70 x 100 = 100 x 70—meaning selling 70 percent of all your seats at 100 percent of their regular value will yield the same gross figure as selling 100 percent of all your seats at 70 percent of their value! So selling a lot of discounts, if your show is not in demand, could help you achieve the gross you need to stay on schedule for recoupment, but it will, of course, lower your average ticket price. Some producers are obsessed with their average ticket price and want it to be as high as possible. The higher the average ticket price, the less its value is being undercut with discounted tickets, indicating the show is a hit and doesn't need to discount. But if your show isn't making any profit, it likely is not much in demand, and I believe fixating on a high average ticket price is false pride in these circumstances. It's a good thing to act like you're a hit, but if the public doesn't believe you, and you persist, it can become delusional! Plus, if one is fortunate enough to market a shaky show into a solid hit, one can always cut off discounts at any time along the way and raise ticket prices when the demand for the show increases. The bottom line is the amount of gross you are making each week and whether or not it enables you to stay open so you can generate enough operating profit to recoup your production expenses within your star(s)'s term(s). Perhaps there is also a philosophical difference in how to best achieve breakeven. In any case, I once fantasized about reporting thusly to my producer:

Me: "I have good news and bad news."
Her: "What's the good news?"
Me: "We have the highest average ticket price on Broadway!"
Her: "That's great! But wait—what's the bad news?"
Me: "We only sold three tickets."

Returning to the recoupment chart, at 80 percent of capacity, recoupment would take under twelve weeks. At 90 percent of capacity, it would take a little over nine weeks. At 100 percent of capacity, one could theoretically recoup in just over seven and a half weeks. I always look carefully at the 70 percent scenario, a realistic and conservative benchmark if one does not have a smash hit, to make sure the term of a star's contract will be sufficient to achieve recoupment at that gross level.

NOTE: In the theater, we always make a big deal about recoupment. A producer once told me about pitching a show he was producing to a relative he hoped would invest. Reviewing a projected recoupment scenario with this relative, the producer proudly explained, "And look, at 70 percent of capacity, you could get your money back in only sixteen weeks!" The relative looked at him bemusedly. "Get it back?" he responded. "Why do I need to get it back? I have it now!" He could also have buried his money in his backyard and dug it up again after sixteen weeks. His point was, he wanted to know what the odds were of his making some *profit* on his money!

In the second scenario titled "Prerecoupment (Net)," an alternative method of paying royalties to the creative team is shown. Instead of paying people a percentage of the gross, which then becomes an additional expense off the top that is *added* to the fixed expenses, the creatives are paid an individually negotiated percentage of net weekly operating profits, that sum of money, if any, *left over* after all the expenses have been paid. If the creatives collectively are entitled to 40 percent of net profits, then the remaining 60 percent of net profits can go to the investors. At a break-even scenario, or worse, in the case of an operating loss, top creatives are simply paid a negotiated, set minimum weekly guarantee, which may or may not be the same guarantee they receive when royalties are calculated on the gross. For this example, let's assume the guarantees are the same in both cases. Above breakeven, each participant would receive his or her percentage of net operating profits—in this example, 22.5 percent for the author, 7.5 percent for the director, and 10 percent for the producer. Each participant would never receive less than his or her minimum guarantee.

Net profit royalty calculations invariably save the show money (i.e., result in lower payouts to the creatives) when the show is performing marginally, either at breakeven or close to it. Compare the two recoupment scenarios that follow the operating budget at the 50 percent capacity level; in each case, the top half or so, up to and including the line for the additional theater percentage, is the same. But with royalties, the collective creative royalties paid out on the net, $38,565, are $7,000 *less* than the collective creative royalties paid on the gross ($45,780), resulting in higher weekly operating profit in the net scenario and therefore a faster recoupment scenario (47.71 weeks versus 54.51 weeks). So why not always calculate royalties based on the net?

Because as the percentage of capacity gross increases, the net royalty calculations invariably *exceed* the gross royalty calculations. Compare the two collective royalty figures in the 100 percent capacity column—they total $91,560 when calculated on the gross and almost twice that, $182,330, when calculated on the net! All creative royalties have to be paid on the same basis—either gross or net—and the collective bargaining agent that governs the working conditions for directors and choreographers, SDC, states that once the producer elects to change the method of calculating royalties from gross to net, that basis must dictate for the remainder of the show's life.

One should therefore consider very carefully before switching to calculating royalties based on the net. Although it may be tempting, in the early days of a show, to lower costs by paying royalties that way, if the show ultimately becomes successful, it is likely this change will saddle the show with higher expenses for the rest of its life!

(Preliminary & Tenative—for Discussion Purposes Only)

Fixed:	335,000	1st Draft: 11/18/16
Prod Costs:	2,760,000	A Broadway Theatre: 1,050 seats

SALARIES

Stars (3 x 20,000, 1 x 4,500)	64,500	estimate of bases
Principals (4 x 2,300)	9,200	
Understudies (4 x 2,250)	9,000	
Stage Managers	5,296	no Term increment
Producers	3,750	
General Manager	3,250	
Company Manager	2,346	
Press Agent	2,513	
Wardrobe (Spvr. + 2)	5,632	
Hair and Make-up (1)	1,464	
Pink Crew	4,400	2 people
Subtotal: 111,351		

DEPARTMENTAL EXPENSE

Stage Manager	200
Carpentry	650
Props/Perishables	150
Electric/Sound	150
Press Agent	300
Rehearsal/Workcall Expense	500
Wardrobe/Costume Replacement/Cleaning	250
Subtotal: 2,200	

RENTALS

Electrics	2,500
Sound	2,500
Automation	3,000
Miscellaneous	500
Subtotal: 8,500	

FIXED ROYALTIES

Author/Director/Producer	0
Set Designer	500
Costume Designer	500
Lighting Designer	500
Sound Designer	500
Composer	500
Casting	750
Fight Director	100
Tech Supervisor	750
Music Rights	450
Subtotal: 4,550	

ADVERTISING & PUBLICITY

Average Advertising Weekly Total	50,000
Additional Amortization	5,000
Marketing Fees	5,500
Marketing Budget	2,500
Other	2,000
Subtotal: 65,000	

THEATER EXPENSE

Rent Gtee/ House Share	15,000
Fixed Operating Charge	15,000
Stagehands (3)	15,000
Other Staff	27,000
House Expenses	18,000
Subtotal: 90,000	

WEEKLY OPERATING BUDGET
(Preliminary & Tenative—for Discussion Purposes Only)

Fixed:	335,000		1st Draft: 11/18/16
Prod Costs:	2,760,000		A Broadway Theatre: 1,050 seats

GENERAL & ADMINISTRATIVE

Producer's Office	1,750	
General Manager's Office	1,250	
Legal	750	
Accounting	1,000	
Insurance	2,000	
Payroll Taxes	7,028	
Union Benefits	9,622	
Vacation/Sick Pay	4,962	
Per Diems	2,100	2 stars
Housing	5,000	2 stars
Car Service	3,000	2 cars
Security	3,000	needed?
Closing Costs (over 16 weeks)	9,000	
Miscellaneous	2,937	
	Subtotal: 53,399	

TOTAL ESTIMATED FIXED EXPENSE	335,000

PRE-RECOUPMENT FULL ROYALTIES

		Av. price $109					Breakeven
		100%	90%	80%	70%	50%	38%
Gross		915,600	824,040	732,480	640,920	457,800	347,873
Fixed (net) **NOT SET YET**		335,000	335,000	335,000	335,000	335,000	335,000
Star 1: $20,000 plus 5% of gross over 375,000		27,030	22,452	17,874	13,296	4,140	0
Star 2: $20,000 plus 5% of gross over 375,000		27,030	22,452	17,874	13,296	4,140	0
Star 3: $20,000 plus 5% of gross over 375,000		27,030	22,452	17,874	13,296	4,140	0
Star 4: n/a		0	0	0	0	0	0
Designer Bumps		3,750	3,750	2,500	1,500	1,500	0
*Theater	6% over $250,000	39,936	34,442	28,949	23,455	12,468	5,872
Author	5.00%	45,780	41,202	36,624	32,046	22,890	2,500
Director	2.00%	18,312	16,481	14,650	12,818	9,156	2,000
Producer	3.00%	27,468	24,721	21,974	19,228	13,734	2,500
	10.00%	91,560	82,404	73,248	64,092	45,780	7,000
PROFIT/(LOSS)		364,264	301,087	239,161	176,985	50,632	0
Number of Weeks to recoup:		7.58	9.17	11.54	15.59	54.51	n/a

PRE-RECOUPMENT (NET)

			Av. price $109					Breakeven
			100%	90%	80%	70%	50%	38%
Gross			915,600	824,040	732,480	640,920	457,800	348,064
Fixed (net) **NOT SET YET**			335,000	335,000	335,000	335,000	335,000	335,000
Star 1: $20,000 plus 5% of gross over 375,000			27,030	22,452	17,874	13,296	4,140	0
Star 2: $20,000 plus 5% of gross over 375,000			27,030	22,452	17,874	13,296	4,140	0
Star 3: $20,000 plus 5% of gross over 375,000			27,030	22,452	17,874	13,296	4,140	0
Star 4: n/a			0	0	0	0	0	0
Designer Bumps			3,750	3,750	2,500	1,500	1,500	0
*Theater	6% over $250,000		39,936	34,442	28,949	23,455	12,468	5,884
PRELIM. PROFIT/(LOSS)			455,824	383,491	312,409	241,077	96,412	7,180
Author	2,500.00	22.500%	102,560	86,286	70,292	54,242	21,693	2,500
Director	2,000.00	7.500%	34,187	28,762	23,431	18,081	7,231	2,000
Producer	2,500.00	10.000%	45,582	38,349	31,241	24,108	24,108	2,500
	7,000.00	40.000%	182,330	153,397	124,964	96,431	38,565	7,000
FINAL PROFIT/(LOSS)			273,494	230,095	187,445	144,646	57,847	180
Number of Weeks to recoup:			10.09	12.00	14.72	19.08	47.71	n/a

***Royalties:

Author	$2,500 gte against 22.5% of weekly net operating profits	22.50%	0.5625
Director	$2,000 gte against 7.5% of weekly net operating profits	7.500%	0.1875
Producer	$2,500 gte against 10% of weekly net operating profits	10.000%	0.2500
		40.000%	1.0000

4

Negotiating Contracts

Prior to becoming a general manager, I spent fourteen years working in a variety of general manager offices, first as an assistant, then as an ATPAM apprentice, and finally as an ATPAM company manager. One general manager I worked for during this time had a very distinctive negotiating style—he would often shout at the person on the other end of the line, slam down the receiver, and, on one memorable occasion, even caused the agent he was negotiating with to cry! When I finally was offered the chance to general manage a Broadway show in 1999, I was unsure if it was necessary to behave this way, or even if I could behave this way. I soon learned that there are many different negotiating styles, all of which can be equally effective. The trick is to find a style that best suits your personality. In my case, being informed, listening carefully, injecting humor into the process, being persuasive, explaining why I couldn't grant a certain request, and proposing fair compromises have proved to be a style that has worked well for me.

NOTE: As an illustration of being persuasive, I once convinced the savvy agent for a multiple award–winning designer to accept a compensation package that was far less than his client's usual Broadway quote. My argument? The script indicated there was no set (which means, really, that there needs to be the *illusion* of no scenery), and since the scope of the work involved was minimal, I reasoned that the designer's fee, advance, and royalty should be too! The agent bought it.

A negotiation is a kind of dance, with each party maneuvering and strategizing to win as much as possible for his side. The best negotiation is one in which, at the end, both parties feel they have won several important points but have not gotten everything they had hoped for. It's important to remember that an agent has to win *something* for her client in order to justify her existence (not to mention her 10 percent commission!) Also, it is much easier for a GM to refuse a particular request if he can say, "Look, I gave you this, I gave you that, but I just can't give in on this point." Of course, it makes a difference if you are negotiating for someone who is young and inexperienced versus someone who is well established and has won major awards. In the first instance, the more the offer represents a major career break, the more likely one is to get the individual for minimum. But what about the second instance, with a successful star in his or her given field, be it acting, directing, or designing?

In this case, the first thing to do, before calling the agent, is your homework! Has this person worked on Broadway before? How recently? How well did that show do financially? If the individual has worked on Broadway recently, chances are an established GM can call a colleague and research that person's last deal. If the star has not had recent Broadway experience, one can always try to research a comparable (in terms of age, awards, and current status within the entertainment industry) star's recent deal. In either event, you will want to strategize your initial offer so that it will not be insultingly low or ignorantly out of sync with what other comparable stars are currently being paid. (Remember, an agent has many clients, or works for an agency that represents many clients, so it is likely the agent will be familiar with a variety of current star deals.)

The most typical negotiation "dance" involves the GM making an opening offer, the agent responding with a counter offer, and the two sides then working toward some kind of compromise. Knowing that an agent will almost certainly try to improve on whatever terms you initially offer, it is smart to open the negotiation by offering terms that are less than what you are prepared to pay. A seasoned agent understands this and will come back with a counter offer significantly higher than what he expects you are willing to pay! With luck, the two of you will wind up meeting in the middle, with you paying exactly what you originally budgeted for, if not less. Much has to do with who needs the other more, or who "has the muscle," as we say in the industry.

I prefer to negotiate, whenever possible, on the phone, actually talking to my counterpart, and keeping detailed notes of our discussion. When that is not practical, email will do, but there is just that much more possibility of one's tone or intention being misunderstood in a one-sided, written communication. On the phone, instant clarification is also possible.

NOTE: When forced to communicate using technology, it's not just an email's tone that could be misunderstood. Sometimes the computer itself can misinterpret and complicate a negotiation conducted by email. I once was hired by a commercial producer to manage the transfer of a play from a nonprofit, Off Broadway theater to Broadway. This is a fairly standard arrangement, involving the commercial producer contributing money to the nonprofit's production, in exchange for obtaining the right of first refusal to subsequently transfer the play, along with its existing physical production, to Broadway if the producer so chooses. I negotiated the basic terms with the nonprofit's attorney, who promised to send me a draft documenting our conversation. When it hadn't arrived after several days, I called to politely inquire. "Oh, I sent you an email later the same day we spoke," she responded. I was surprised, as I get hundreds of emails a day and rarely leave the office without reviewing that day's correspondence. I hunted for her email and eventually found it in my junk mail, where I don't usually look. She suggested I send her an email, so our computers would recognize each other, which I promptly did. We then reviewed her draft, I requested a few changes, she said she'd incorporate them and send me a revised copy, and we hung up. When I hadn't received anything from her in several days, I called to politely inquire again. "I sent it the same day we spoke," she said. "Did you look in your junk mail?" I hadn't, but did, and there was her email. "I don't understand why this is happening," I said. "Maybe there's an issue with something in the subject line?" she offered. "Right," said I, "what could there possibly be—" and cut myself off with a gasp of comprehension. This kind of document has a standard name, which was referenced in the subject line of all our correspondence; it is called an enhancement agreement! Clearly, my computer thought we were carrying on a smutty correspondence involving the enlargement of private body parts!

In resolving differences, always strive to protect the show at breakeven, or close thereto, for as long as possible. As previously discussed, a show can run forever as long as it can cover its expenses. If an agent wants his or her client to receive more money than you want to pay as part of your base fixed expenses, there are ways to delay some of the compensation and transfer it to a variable expense, triggered by higher gross thresholds when the show can better afford it. This will be discussed in further detail in reviewing some of the actual contracts that follow.

From an ego standpoint, most stars, if not their agents, want to be reassured that nobody is getting a better deal than they are. Thus, if you have multiple stars in a show, a valuable negotiating device is to offer them terms that are on a **favored nations** basis with each other—everyone at a certain level receiving the exact same deal. This can often be restricted to certain areas, chiefly financial compensation, but may also include terms for such areas as billing, length of term, house seats, opening night tickets, approved absences to accommodate outside employment, and car service. Conversely, other areas can be excluded from favored nations—like transportation, housing, and per diem—that may not apply to actors who live in New York City but need to be addressed with actors brought in from out of town. Amazingly, people will often agree to work for less as long as they are convinced no one else is getting more!

NOTE: I once witnessed this psychology applied with what I felt was bizarre logic, essentially cutting off one's nose to spite one's face. I was managing a workshop of a new musical that was heading to Broadway. The same individual was the author, director, and producer, so he was spread pretty thin wearing three different hats. He decided it would be useful to him as the author to videotape the presentation that was occurring at the end of the workshop. This way, he could have something to study and learn from that might assist him in doing rewrites. This is not normally allowed, so I inquired from Equity if we would be permitted to film the presentation, assuring them that the recording would be used for archival purposes only and that it would not be exploited for any commercial gain. Equity replied that we would have to ask our company, and if they unanimously agreed, and if we paid them all the same additional **SAG/AFTRA (Screen Actors Guild/American Federation of Television and Radio Artists)** fee to record the presentation, Equity would allow it. I also researched the SAG/AFTRA status of all our cast members and discovered some were already SAG/AFTRA members, some were not and would have to join, requiring an initiation fee, and some were members but were delinquent in their dues, which would have to be paid up in full before they could be reinstated as members in good standing.

I went back to the producer and explained the situation to him. I also mentioned, since taping the show was primarily of interest to him, that I felt it was unlikely that those company members who did not already belong to SAG/AFTRA or were delinquent in their dues would agree to the plan, as it would entail a personal expense for them. I suggested he offer to pay for these expenses himself, so that no actor would be out of pocket. He generously consented. Thus, I could tell our company that if they all agreed, everyone would get paid the same additional filming fee for no additional work (they were going to do the presentation anyway, whether it was filmed or not), it wouldn't cost anyone anything, and everyone would wind up a fully paid member of a sister performing union, through which he or she might be able to get future employment. I thought it was a slam dunk, no-brainer, sure thing.

I told the stage manager to tell the actors there would be a brief company meeting following rehearsal that day and laid out the details for them. I explained that the decision to tape or not was up to them and had to be unanimous, but if they agreed, they would all be receiving additional money and no one would be out of pocket. I then proposed that I should leave, allowing them to deliberate in private, and promised to return the next day for their decision.

When I did return, one actor in the company had been selected to be the spokesperson. It so happened that he was the only cast member who was currently appearing in a Broadway show, was making good money, and was one of the few performers who was already a fully paid-up member of SAG/AFTRA. He explained to me that they had all talked, and because the essence of the workshop contract was favored nations, their consensus was that it wasn't fair that some members of the group would have their initiation fees, or back dues, paid for them, a financial benefit that not all of them would be receiving. No one had paid for *their* initiation fees; they'd had to pay for it all themselves. Therefore, they would only agree to the taping if those who were already members were *reimbursed* for their initiation fees! I explained to him that this additional expense might well convince the producer to scratch the idea, in which case they would all lose out on receiving the additional taping fee, which, I stressed again, required no additional work. It made no difference. He had singlehandedly convinced the company that this was the principled stand to take and clearly couldn't tolerate seeing anyone else receive a benefit he hadn't received. Guess what? The producer decided not to tape the workshop.

In a protracted negotiation, some agents will try to wear you down and will push for as much as they can get for as long as they can. If the agent keeps insisting his client requires a higher base salary than you have budgeted for, you can always tell him that you don't know if that will be possible, but you will go back to the producer and relay the request. (This can also be used as a stalling tactic, to make the other side nervous that they may be blowing the deal and should back down from their demand.) The producer can then either approve the over budget request or tell the GM to draw the line and say to the agent, "I've really tried to accommodate you and give as much as I can, but the budget simply won't allow for more. This is our final offer, take it or leave it. I need your reply by 5 p.m. tomorrow, or we are rescinding our offer and moving on." Again, never issue such an ultimatum without your producer's prior approval! And be sure you mean it when you say it. Sometimes one party simply requires more than the other can afford to pay, and, regrettably, you do have to move on. It's not personal, it's business.

The following chapters contain a variety of sample "star" contracts used on Broadway—for an actor, a director, a designer, and a general manager. What one thinks of as the contract, the document containing all of the substantive, negotiated, above-minimum terms of employment, is actually a multipage *rider* to the collective bargaining agreement for the applicable union. The negotiated rider is attached to the applicable single-sheet union contract face form—issued by Actors' Equity Association (AEA) for an actor or stage manager, by Stage Directors and Choreographers Society (SDC) for a director or choreographer, or by United Scenic Artists (USA) for a designer. (General managers do not have a union, although company managers belong to ATPAM.) Often when an individual has achieved a certain level of success, he or she will set up a loan-out company for tax-related reasons, which provides the services of the individual. The company acts as a "Lender f/s/o . . ." (for the services of) the individual. This loan-out company is paid a fee and, in turn, pays the salary of the individual. In this event, there is boilerplate language at the end of the contract rider that links the obligations and services of the lender/company to those of the individual.

Finally, I would like to mention that there are two very important contracts a GM usually reviews, comments on, and/or negotiates but does not himself generate—the author's option agreement, traditionally negotiated by the production attorney, and the theater license agreement, the template for which is provided by the theater owner. Because neither are the intellectual property of the GM, they are not included among the contract samples discussed here.

5

Sample Star Actor Contract Rider

Riders disclose any negotiated terms that exceed the minimum terms stated in the applicable union agreement that has jurisdiction over a contract. For actors and stage managers, this union is Actors' Equity Association (AEA or Equity). Aside from providing for a higher level of compensation, a star actor's contract will likely contain special clauses in such areas as transportation, housing and per diem (if applicable), billing, car service, security, photo approval, make-up and hair styling allowance (for publicity appearances), house seats, opening night tickets and party invitation allowance, choice of dressing room, position of bio in the program, right to an exclusive dresser, "out" clauses to accept other employment during the course of the term, length of term, vacation provisions, and liability insurance coverage, to name a few. Sometimes a star contract is accompanied by a confidential side letter that contains additional terms that are not shared with the union, as the items discussed are outside of the union's jurisdiction. The following sample contract rider will give you a good idea of the kind of negotiated issues that are typically included in, and form the core of, a star actor's contract.

RIDER TO ACTORS' EQUITY STANDARD TERM PRODUCTION CONTRACT DATED AS OF _____ BETWEEN _____ (star loanout corporation) (Fed ID #_____) (LENDER) f/s/o _____ (ACTOR) AND _____ (Name of Broadway LP or LLC) (PRODUCER) WITH RESPECT TO THE PRODUCTION OF "_____" (PLAY) AT THE _____ THEATER IN NEW YORK CITY.

Whenever and wherever the provisions of this Rider differ from or conflict with the printed portion of this contract, the provisions of this Rider shall prevail.

1. **REPORT DATE/PRODUCTION SCHEDULE:** Lender agrees to cause Actor to report for rehearsal in New York City on or about (but no earlier than, unless Actor otherwise agrees in writing) _____. The current production schedule is as follows:

New York rehearsal: on or about _____
New York tech: on or about _____
First New York performance: on or about _____
Opening Night: on or about _____

Producer agrees to give Lender reasonably prompt notice, but in any event not less than 15 days advance notice, of any change in rehearsal report date.

NOTE: Dates can shift for a variety of reasons, which is why it is advisable to qualify them with the phrase "on or about."

2. **TERM.** This contract shall be for seventeen and a half (17½) playing weeks, beginning with the first New York performance, with Thanksgiving Day off and an unpaid Christmas hiatus of December 20–25 inclusive, per rule 38 A (1), except that:

a) Producer may terminate this Contract by giving one (1) week written company closing notice to Actor (with a copy to _____ (agency) attn: _____ (agent); and

b) In any event, this Contract shall terminate on _____.

78

No other cast member shall have a shorter contractual time commitment or be entitled to receive "outs" or vacations during the production period for the Play, with the possible exception of unanticipated emergency or family need, or as allowed per Rule 32 (F), (G), and (H) of the Actors' Equity Association Equity/League Production Contract.

Actor will play any and all public or religious holidays as requested by Producer, except as noted above.

NOTE: Seventeen and a half playing weeks was the longest we could secure the services of this star. Reviewing the show's recoupment scenarios, I made sure it was theoretically possible to recoup during this term at 70 percent of capacity. Shows often change their regular playing schedules to accommodate major holidays. Here we replaced the Thanksgiving Thursday evening performance with a special Friday afternoon matinee, which is standard. The star wanted some time off to celebrate Christmas with her family; we accommodated by giving her the five days leading up to, and including, Christmas Day itself, which is normally a slow period business-wise. We made sure to be playing for the remainder of the holidays, from the day after Christmas through the weekend following New Year's Day, which is one of the most lucrative periods of the entire year. Note that if we designate this lay-off in performances prior to Christmas in all of the Equity members' contract riders, as I do here, then the show is not required to pay any salaries during the hiatus. Finally, note how the star's agent wanted to make sure no one else had cushier terms of employment in terms of shorter length of term, "outs" (prenegotiated, acceptable conditions for missing performances), or a vacation, which ordinarily would not be considered before at least six months of employment had transpired.

3. **COMPENSATION.** For the term of Actor's engagement hereunder, Producer agrees to pay Lender and each of Lender and Actor agrees to accept as compensation hereunder the following amounts:

a) For rehearsals: Actors' Equity Production Contract applicable minimum, currently _____ (_____) dollars a week plus a two percent (2%) Media Fee ($_____), for a total of _____ ($_____) dollars a week, which shall be on a favored nations basis with the entire cast.

b) For all paid public performances in New York City: a guarantee of fifteen thousand ($15,000) dollars per week, prorated on the basis of eight (8) performances a week, which shall include the 2% Media Fee and a Term increment.

c) Additional Compensation based on percentage of gross weekly box office receipts (GWBOR): 5% of GWBOR from $300,000 per week to less than $400,000 per week, 2.5% of GWBOR from $400,000 per week and over. By way of example, if the GWBOR was $600,000, Actor would receive an additional $5,000 for the GWBOR between $300,000 and $400,000, and an additional $5,000 for 2.5% of the $200,000 above $400,000. The foregoing benchmarks determining when Actor will receive a percentage of GWBOR shall be adjusted proportionately for performance weeks with fewer than eight (8) performances. (By way of example, for a week in which there are only four (4) performances the benchmarks would be reduced by 50%, and Actor's percentage of GWBOR shall be: 5% of GWBOR from $150,000 per week to less than $200,000 per week, and 2.5% of GWBOR from $200,000 per week and over. Further by way of example, if the GWBOR in a 4-performance week is $300,000, Actor would receive an additional $2,500 for the GWBOR between $150,000 and $200,000, and an additional $2,500 for 2.5% of the $100,000 GWBOR above $200,000.) The definition of GWBOR shall be as per the Dramatists Guild Approved Production Contract, applicable to all royalty participants, including author, director, producer, and all other performers.

NOTE: *This star's agent wanted his client to receive a total compensation package of $25,000/week. Upon investigation, I discovered the agent was willing to get his client to that sum, but the show didn't necessarily have to guarantee that full amount at breakeven or thereabouts. Remember—always try to protect the show at the low end of operating! One option was to offer a guarantee of a lower amount initially, subsequently rising in steps over time—only so much money through the first six performance weeks (or even better, through the first six full performance weeks following opening night!), rising to a higher sum for weeks seven through twelve, rising again to an even higher sum from week thirteen on. The theory is that if you can buy time, and the show is still running, it has probably become established in the marketplace, is performing well, and can afford to increase its fixed operating costs. Even better, as I did here, you might offer a lower* *guaranteed amount ($15,000 here, $10,000 less than the desired goal of $25,000) plus an additional percentage of the gross beginning at a specified gross threshold; this way, you can pay the star more as the show makes more money, when you know you can afford it. If negotiating in this direction, it is preferable (for the show!) to have the star's percentage be in addition to her guarantee and for it to kick in at a gross threshold a little bit above breakeven, rather than have the guarantee be against her percentage. You can always tell the agent, "Look, if your client is really the draw you say she is and is pulling them in, at a gross of X she will be making $25,000 a week!" Here you are asking the star to prove her value and earn her star salary.*

Other means of providing stars with additional compensation, but delaying it until you are confident the show can afford it rather than encumbering the show early on, include offering a bump in their weekly guarantee after the show has recouped or, occasionally, awarding stars a percentage of net profits. This last should be discouraged, as it comes off the top, thereby diminishing the amount of adjusted net profits that are then split between the investors and the producer(s).

4. **BILLING.** Actor shall receive above the title billing in first position in one of the following three configurations:

Star First Name   Costar First Name
Star Last Name   Costar Second Name

OR

Star Name
Costar Name

OR

Star Name Costar Name

in

NAME OF PLAY HERE

Said credit shall be one hundred (100%) percent of the size of the type used for the title of the Play, over the title, in the same size and style of type for all performers, as set forth in the three billing alternatives above. Subject to these formats, Actor shall receive no less favorable billing entitlements with respect to artwork/likeness/paid ad/excluded ad (under a certain size, etc.) than any other performer, including front-of-house displays, marquees, and ABCs.

Actor's billing will appear wherever credit is accorded any other person in connection with the Play (including but not limited to any other cast member, the director, and/or the author), excluding award/congratulatory ads naming only the person(s) lauded and critics' quotes and institutional ads that do not mention any other actor. No person or entity will receive larger or more prominent billing than Actor. Actor will be cited in "critics quotes" in paid ads controlled by Producer, either in the same ad or in an equivalent number of similarly placed ads, provided appropriate favorable quotes for Actor are reasonably available.

Wherever credits are accorded in connection with the Play in a so-called "billing box" pursuant to which Actor is entitled to credit, the size of Actor's credit in said "billing box" shall be determined by the size of the title in the billing box. If Actor's name shall also appear as part of the artwork/logo for the Play, it shall always appear in 100% size of the title of Play that appears in said artwork/logo.

Actor's name shall appear in accordance with the terms set forth in this paragraph 4, i.e., as to position, size in all advertising, including all *New York Times* "ABCs".

NOTE: *Working out a star's billing is a big part of his contract. A lot of ego is invested in the billing terms—how large the credit is (100% of title is standard for a star), where it appears (above the title, below the title, last but preceded by the word "and," within a box, following the phrase "also starring," etc.), what order it appears in (the biggest star usually gets top, or first, billing), making sure no one else has bigger billing, gets more quotes in ads, has a bigger presence outside the theater, etc. One of the most famous billing disputes in the history of theater occurred in 1936, when both Ethel Merman's and Jimmy Durante's agents insisted their client deserved top billing in Cole Porters's* Red, Hot and Blue! *The ultimate solution? Both stars had their name in its own box, equal in size to each other, and the two boxes criss-crossed each other diagonally—Durante's started at upper left and descended towards bottom right, and the Merm's started at bottom left and ascended toward upper right! As we need to remind ourselves at times, most billing issues, thankfully, can be resolved with ink, not bucks.*

In the theater, billing someone above the title confers "star" status on him and qualifies him to be considered for a Tony Award nomination in the Leading Actor category. But this can prove to be a trap. I once general managed a stage adaptation of Ivan Turgenev's Fortunes Fool, *in which both Alan Bates and Frank Langella were billed above the title and gave Tony-worthy performances. We were concerned that both of them would be nominated and wind up competing against each other, so, after consulting with my producers and Frank's agent, who understood the dilemma, I preemptively petitioned the Tony committee. I made a compelling case, the gist of which was that Frank, although billed above the title as befitted an actor of his status, should be considered in the Featured Actor category, as the size of his role was more appropriate to that classification. Happily, the Tony administrative committee agreed, both actors were nominated in their respective categories, and both wound up winning best actor Tony Awards that year!*

5. **TELEVISION/RADIO COMMERCIAL.** In the event Producer shall elect to produce a television or radio commercial in connection with the Play, Actor agrees at reasonably scheduled times and locations and, subject to Actor's availability, to render services in such commercial, if required by Producer, for the applicable union minimum scale, assuming no one else receives more than scale. In addition, Actor agrees to allow Producer to use footage (as reasonably approved in advance by Actor) from any documentaries on the Play for purposes of promoting Play in any of the Equity-approved venues detailed in rule 39, Media, Promotion and Publicity, in return for Actor receiving a single AFTRA/SAG fee, such fee to be on a favored nations basis with all other persons appearing in such footage.

NOTE: *Basic boilerplate. Assures that the actor, if the producer so elects, will make a commercial for minimum and allow the footage to be used as per Equity's guidelines, on a favored nations basis with the rest of the cast.*

6. **STAGE BUSINESS.** It is hereby agreed that any material whatsoever including but not limited to any form of stage business performed or contributed by Actor in rehearsal or any performance of the Play shall, insofar as Actor is concerned, be the property of the Producer of the Play.

NOTE: Boilerplate. What evolves out of the rehearsal process or in performance becomes part of the play and is the producer's property.

7. **ADDITIONAL DUTIES.** The weekly compensation provided to be paid to Actor in this contract and Rider insofar as it exceeds AEA minimums shall be inclusive of any and all amounts deemed payable to Actor pursuant to Actors' Equity Association rules for Additional Duties including but not limited to Term, Extraordinary Risk, Stunt, Scenic and Prop Moves, Fight Captain, Media Fee, or any other duties.

NOTE: It is important to include this clause so that if you are paying an actor a salary that is over scale (minimum), that extra amount can double as payment for these union-required premiums. If you omit this language, each additional duty required by you will trigger even more payments on top of the actor's already over-scale salary!

8. **RENDER SERVICES.** Actor shall not render any services in connection with or perform in any way material written for or contained in the Play, on Actor's own behalf or on the behalf of anyone other than the Producer, or for any purpose whatsoever other than as part of the performance of Actor's role in the Play, hereunder, without the written consent of the Producer, not to be unreasonably withheld. The foregoing shall be in effect for the duration of the Term of Actor's Agreement hereunder.

NOTE: Boilerplate.

9. **NO CONFLICT.** Actor represents and warrants that Actor has not heretofore entered into any contract or undertaken any commitment and will not hereafter do so in conflict with the foregoing, and acknowledges that Actor shall render Actor's services in the Play, as required hereunder, to the best of Actor's ability. The foregoing notwithstanding, Producer acknowledges that Actor has received permission to attend _____ (description of immediate family member's life event) on _____ (date), and will therefore be unable to perform the matinee and evening performances on that date.

NOTE: This is where you should identify any preexisting performance conflicts the actor expects to have during the course of his or her term (like an immediate family member's wedding) and acknowledge that, as a consequence, the actor will miss a specified number of performances and not receive any salary while he or she is not providing services. If such conflicts exist, they can prove useful when hiring the understudy for this role, as you can tell the agent you are giving him advance notice that his client will be performing the role on such and such a date. With advance notice, the understudy can work to get casting agents, as well as family and friends, to see his performance.

10. **PUBLICITY.** Actor shall comply with all reasonable publicity requests, subject to the following terms:

Actor shall, at Producer's request, make herself available at mutually agreeable times for a reasonable and customary number of show-related publicity requests, including but not limited to interviews for newspapers, magazines, and other publications and appearances on radio and television, in connection with the promotion and publicizing of the Play. In connection with all such requests, Producer will make car service available for Actor to attend publicity-related functions (such car service to conform to the provisions of paragraph 15 below, with the exception of the 8 hours of waiting time, it being understood waiting time for such publicity services will not be charged against Actor's personal to and from home to theater 8 hours of weekly waiting time).

Actor shall have the right to reject any individual publicity requests under this paragraph 10 so long as actor accepts a reasonable and customary amount of star publicity in aggregate during her engagement in the Play.

Actor shall have mutually agreed professional hair/make-up for all publicity events/appearances, with caps of $300 for hair and $300 for make-up. Such caps will be no less favorable than for any other actor in the Play during the term of Actor's engagement therein.

Actor will have the right of approval of all photographs containing Actor's likeness used to publicize or advertise the Play as per the following guidelines: for individual shots, Actor hereby agrees to approve at least fifty (50%) percent of the shots submitted to her; for group shots with other cast having photo approval, Actor hereby agrees to approve at least seventy-five (75%) percent of the shots submitted to her. Photos will be submitted to Actor in reasonable quantity.

Actor will have up to three (3) "passes" on any nonphotographic likeness for Actor used in connection with the Play before a likeness shall be deemed to be approved.

Producer shall have the right to use Actor's name, approved likeness, and approved bio material in connection with the Play, its production, promotion, and presentation, but not in commercial tie-ins, sponsorships, or in any manner indicating Actor endorses any product, service, entity, or cause unless Actor otherwise agrees in writing. Actor's approved bio will appear in first position of all bios in the program or *Playbill*. Pursuant to Equity rules, and subject to Actor's right of reasonable approval of material featuring her and so used, Producer may permit the use of excerpts from the Play in which Actor appears on entertainment, interview, magazine format, talk show, and awards programs, but only through the end of Actor's engagement in the Play hereunder.

NOTE: A producer relies on the star to help promote the show. Therefore, it is imperative that all the terms related to this publicity are prenegotiated and clearly stated in the contract.

11. **DRESSING ROOM.** Actor shall have first choice of a private dressing room, with customary Broadway Theatre amenities (subject to architecture of the Theater) including a private telephone, if desired, half refrigerator, and couch. Producer agrees to pay for the installation of the telephone and for all local calls; Actor and/or Lender as applicable shall be responsible for Actor's own long-distance telephone charges.

NOTE: This is all fairly standard language for a star. Note this star has been given the right to first choice of dressing rooms. Make sure you give this right to your main star or, if there are more than one, to the first one to sign a contract.

12. **HOUSE SEATS.** For each and every performance of the Play produced by Producer, Producer shall cause two (2) adjoining pairs of center orchestra seats in the fourth through tenth rows to be held for purchase by Actor or Actor's designee at regular box office prices, reducible to one (1) pair

for theater party, press performances, Tony voter, or benefit performances if all other cast's house seat holds are also so reduced. Per Producer's contract with the theater owner, such tickets shall be held until ninety-six (96) hours in advance of each performance. Actor's house seats will be held and maintained by the Play's General Manager's office, who agrees to keep such books and records as may be required for Producer to comply with the rules and regulations of the Attorney General of the State of New York or any other governmental agency having jurisdiction. Producer shall make best efforts to accommodate Actor's house seat needs when more than four seats are required for any one performance, or when less than ninety-six (96) hours notice is given. No other actor shall receive more favorable house seat terms.

NOTE: House seats *(choice location seats specifically reserved for a top creative's personal use, and therefore not on sale to the general public— when a show advertises it is sold out, the stars, author, director, producer, GM, designers, press agent, and theater owner will still have access to a pool of choice seats available only to them) are also often a matter of ego—terms will typically include how many, where they are located (what row, or range of rows, whether they are in the center or side section, if pairs need to be adjacent), if they are reducible in number for specified occasions, as well as the assurance that no one else has better terms.*

13. **OFFICIAL PRESS OPENING.** For the Official Press Opening Night performance of the Broadway Production, Actor shall be entitled to receive, at no charge, 5 pairs of seats in good orchestra locations and 11 party invitations to the opening night party. Actor shall be entitled to purchase additional seats and tickets to the party as needed. Actor shall have reserved table(s) at the opening night party to accommodate all of Actor's guests.

NOTE: *The number of opening night seats granted varies from show to show and will reflect how important the star is, how many other stars the show has, how large the cast is, how large the theater is, how large a family the star has, etc.*

14. PAYMENT. Producer shall pay Actor in the name of her corporation and send such amounts of Actor's salary as instructed by Actor or Actor's agent to:

_____

_____

_____

Attn: _____

Or as otherwise instructed jointly in writing by Agent and Lender/Actor.

NOTE: Most stars do not have their weekly salary handed to them. Instead, it is usually sent on their behalf to their agent, their manager, their business manager, or their attorney, who deposits it for them. This is a good thing. I once worked on a show with a very talented, rather ethereal young star. One day, the company manager came in to the office and said, "You're not going to believe what happened last night! I got to the theater and the treasurer said, 'Hey, Miriam (not the CM's real name), Amelia (not the star's real name) is looking for you.' So I went up to her dressing room and we had the following exchange:

M: *"Yes, Amelia. How can I help you?"*

B: *"Oh, Miriam, I went out last night after the show, must have had too much to drink, and got separated from my purse. I'm afraid there were several paychecks in it."*

M: *"Several! How many, Amelia?"*

B: *"Oh, I don't know, three or four . . ."*

M: *"Three or four!"*

B: *"Yes, but don't worry, no one can cash them. I already signed my name on the back."*

15. CAR SERVICE. Producer shall provide Actor with first-class exclusive sedan car service to and from Actor's Manhattan apartment and the theater for technical/dress rehearsals, performances, and show-related publicity appearances, including eight (8) hours of wait time per week, such wait time not to be carried forward to a later week if it is not used. Producer shall also provide Actor with a car on opening night through the after party. Actor and Producer shall have mutual approval of car service and driver(s), not to be unreasonably withheld, and Producer shall exert reasonable efforts, to the greatest possible extent, to provide Actor with the same driver daily.

NOTE: *This is standard language for car service. Note the producer is granting the actor eight hours of free wait time per week, as a star often has to greet guests backstage or sign autographs outside the stage door and should not be penalized for doing either.*

16. **HAIRSTYLE.** Producer and Actor agree to mutual shared approval over any change in Actor's hairstyle required by the hair design of Play, including but not limited to wearing a wig or a change in the color of Actor's hair and/or the cutting or growing of Actor's hair. Producer agrees to pay for the original expense of such change, the expense of the upkeep of said hair or hairstyle during Actor's term hereunder (including the maintenance of Actor's own hair supposing no change is required by the design of the Play), and the cost to restore Actor's original hair color at the close of Actor's engagement. Any work required to be done will be done by a stylist mutually approved by Actor and Producer.

NOTE: *Again, this is standard language. A star needs to be assured that any changes required to her hair will be mutual, that is, she has to agree to them as well, and she will have approval over the person making any such changes.*

17. **INDEMNITY.** Producer will defend and indemnify Lender and Actor from and against all claims, liabilities, costs and damages (including outside attorneys' fees and costs), or litigation made in respect of the development, production, performance, and or exploitation of the Play hereunder and/or this Agreement, other than damages caused by (a) tortious act of Actor and/or Lender or (b) breach by Actor and/or Lender of their respective representations, warranties, and/or agreements hereunder.

If Producer secures any errors and omissions and/or general liability insurance policy covering the production of the Play hereunder (it being understood Producer is under no obligation to secure such insurance), Producer will cause Actor and Actor's loan-out company to be covered as additional insured parties under each such policy.

NOTE: *Boilerplate. Remember that the producer has insurance obligations to the star; this will be discussed further in chapter 12.*

18. **PERFORMANCE SCHEDULE.** Producer hereby informs Actor that the Play will have a regular performance schedule of Tuesday evenings at 7 p.m., Wednesday through Saturday evenings at 8 p.m., with matinees Wednesday and Saturday at 2 p.m., and Sunday at 3 p.m. During the course of Actor's term, there may be alterations in the regular weekly schedule to accommodate critics performances or special holiday concerns.

No principal performer in the Play shall be given the contractual right to play fewer than eight (8) performances in a week.

NOTE: *On Broadway, most shows play either a Monday to Saturday schedule, with Sundays off, or a Tuesday to Sunday schedule, with Mondays off. As a courtesy, this paragraph informs the actor which option the producer has initially chosen, indicates that he or she will play four shows between Friday night and Sunday afternoon, and that this schedule is subject to change at the producer's election.*

19. **STUNT.** Per Actors' Equity Rule 62 I, Actor is hereby notified that Actor will be involved in the performance of a stunt.

NOTE: *Per the Equity rulebook, if the producer hires a stunt coordinator to teach a stunt, then the producer must notify the actor(s) involved in a contract rider, as well as notify Equity prior to the rehearsal or performance of the stunt.*

20. **EXTRAORDINARY RISK.** This shall serve as notice that Actor shall perform _____ (describe action here) that Equity deems to be an Extraordinary Risk, payment for which is covered under paragraph 7, ADDITIONAL DUTIES, hereinabove.

NOTE: *Equity defines Extraordinary Risk as performing acrobatic feats; suspension from trapezes, wires, or like contrivances; the use of or exposure to weapons, fire, or pyrotechnic devices; and the taking of dangerous leaps, falls, throws, catches, knee drops, or slides. Extraordinary risks must* *be identified in a contract rider and require an additional payment of $20/ week, unless the contract specifically states, as it does here in paragraph 7, that the payment for this additional duty is covered by the over-scale salary the actor is receiving.*

21. **HOUSING.** Producer shall provide Actor with a mutually approved one-bedroom rental apartment in New York City, commencing one week prior to the start of rehearsals and continuing until three days following the end of the run of the Play. Should the run of the Play end earlier than anticipated, Producer shall be responsible for any rent due on Actor's rental apartment until such time as Producer can terminate Producer's rental agreement with the rental agent.

NOTE: Fairly standard housing language. Whenever possible, it is in the show's interest to convince the star to stay in a hotel rather than an apartment, as a hotel will not involve a real estate broker's fee or the amount of complicated paperwork that a rental in a co-op or condo entails, not to mention obtaining board approval. Also, never commit an actor to an apartment before he or she has seen it in person and approved it. This may mean putting the actor up in a hotel for a few days when he first comes into town, so you can show him a variety of properties that have been lined up for review. Finally, it is reasonable to allow the actor to stay in his apartment for a few days following the close of the show.

22. **PER DIEM.** Producer agrees to pay Actor a per diem of $100 inclusive of travel and hold days, on a favored nations basis with Actor's costar.

NOTE: An accepted, but not lavish, amount to pay a star just for her food expenses. Remember, a per diem of $100 translates to $700 weekly.

23. **TRANSPORTATION.** Producer agrees to supply Actor with round trip, first-class airfare between Los Angeles and New York City and to reimburse Actor for any ground transportation to and from the airport connected thereto.

NOTE: Standard language. It is highly unlikely you will be able to get a star to travel in business class. Sometimes a star has a lot of mileage points accumulated and requests the cash equivalent of his airfare in exchange for arranging his own travel.

24. **DRESSER.** Actor shall have her own exclusive Dresser. Actor hereby approves _____.

NOTE: *Most stars will require their own dresser. This person not only helps them with costume changes but looks after and coddles them—he or she may get them warm tea from the green room, run out and bring them back a sandwich from the neighborhood deli, greet the star's backstage guests and escort them to a holding area, etc.*

25. **TONY AWARD® BONUS.** If Actor wins a Tony Award as Best Actor, Producer will pay Actor a one-time bonus of $20,000 within one week after the date of the award.

NOTE: *If the actor will still be under contract when the Tony Awards occur (normally held the first or second Sunday in June), you should include this language here. If, however, the actor's term will have ended and he or she will no longer be under contract, you may choose to put this provision in a side letter.*

LOAN OUT NAME F/S/O   BROADWAY ENTITY
ACTOR (LENDER)

_____   _____

by: _____ (ACTOR)   by: _____ General Manager

RIDER TO ACTORS' EQUITY STANDARD TERM PRODUCTION CONTRACT FOR _____ f/s/o _____ (CONTRACTOR) BETWEEN _____ (PRODUCER) AND _____ (ACTOR) FOR "_____" (PLAY). THIS RIDER DATED _____.

Whenever and wherever the provisions of this Rider differ from or conflict with the printed portion of this contract, the provisions of this Rider shall prevail.

1. It is understood and agreed that all references to Actor in the contract and Rider dated as of _____ shall be applicable to Contractor.

2. Contractor acknowledges that it is executing this contract as an independent contractor and shall perform and discharge all obligations imposed under all Federal, State, or local laws, orders, and regulations in connection with the services of the Actor furnished by Contractor to the Producer. Contractor further agrees that the Actor shall be and remain during the Term hereof a member of Actors' Equity Association and will perform services hereunder in accordance with the terms and conditions of Actors' Equity Association Standard Term Production Contract for Broadway Productions. Contractor and Producer agree that the rules and regulations of Actors' Equity Association shall be applicable as they may apply to this Contract, and agree respectively to comply with such rules and regulations and the terms of the attached Actors' Equity Association Standard Term Production Contract for Broadway Productions and Rider as they apply.

3. The Producer agrees to make Pension and Welfare payments on the gross weekly payments for the services of Actor stated herein with Equity Rules as they may apply and to make additional payments which may be due or become due the Actor pursuant to Equity regulations as they may apply to this Contract.

_____ INC. BROADWAY ENTITY

f/s/o _____

by:_____   by:_____
CONTRACTOR   GENERAL MANAGER
Fed ID # _____

NOTE: *The text on the previous page is boilerplate language when an actor is employed through his own loan-out corporation.*

Gentlemen:

In order to induce you to enter into the Agreement dated as of
_____ herewith with _____ f/s/o
_____ ("Contractor") for the rendering of my ser-
vices as performer with respect to the stage play presently entitled
"_____" (the "Play"), and in consideration of your execution and delivery thereof, I hereby:

1. Warrant that the Contractor is and will at all times be entitled to enter
into the said Agreement and make available my services to you in accordance with the said Agreement;

2. Agree that if Contractor should be dissolved or should otherwise cease
to exist or for any reason whatsoever should fail, be unable, neglect, or
refuse to duly perform and observe or procure the performance and obser-
vance of each and all of the terms and conditions of the said Agreement,
I shall, at your election, be deemed added as a direct party to the said
Agreement, jointly and severally with Contractor, without prejudice to any
rights you may have against Contractor and further without prejudice to
my undertaking under paragraph 3 below;

3. Undertake to look solely to the Contractor for all compensation for
my services to be rendered under the said Agreement and not in any event
to look to you for such compensation or any part thereof unless the con-
tingency referred to in paragraph 2 hereof shall occur, in which event
you shall thereafter pay me directly the money you agree to pay to the
Contractor under the Agreement;

4. Undertake that no breach by the Contractor of any of its obligations to
me shall constitute or be deemed to constitute a breach by you under the
said Agreement and accordingly, notwithstanding such breach, I undertake
to continue to fulfill all of my obligations hereunder if and so long as you
fulfill your obligations to the Contractor;

5. Agree that any notice served on the Contractor in accordance with the terms of the said Agreement shall be deemed to be notice to me.

6. I acknowledge that to the best of my knowledge in the exercise of reasonable prudence, I am under no disability which would interfere with my full compliance with the Contract.

Very truly yours,   Accepted and agreed to:
                                                     BROADWAY ENTITY

_____   By: _____
ACTOR _____   _____, General Manager

NOTE: *Boilerplate language when an actor is employed through his own loan-out corporation.*

SIDE LETTER NOT TO BE SHARED WITH ACTOR'S UNION

BROADWAY ENTITY
c/o GM Office
Street Address
New York, NY 100__
Tel.: ; Fax: ; E-mail:

Date

Loanout f/s/o Actor
c/o Agent
Agency
Street Address
City, State Zip

RE: NAME OF PLAY

Dear _____ (Name of Actor):

This will confirm that we have agreed to the following in addition to the terms and conditions in the annexed AEA Rider of this date between _____ (Producer) and _____ (Lender) f/s/o _____ (Actor).

1. Due to the physical demands of Actor's role, Actor will receive a one-time-only allowance of $3,000 for a trainer. Actor will be promptly reimbursed for this expense upon presentation of an invoice to Producer.

2. Producer shall pay for Actor's visit to a physical therapist once a month during the rehearsal and performance period. Actor will be promptly reimbursed for this expense upon presentation of an invoice to Producer.

3. Producer shall provide Actor's assistant with one round trip coach airline ticket between Los Angeles and New York on a carrier such as Jet Blue.

4. Producer agrees to pay Actor's assistant, _____, a weekly fee of $250/week, prorated on the basis of an eight (8) performance week, beginning with the first week of rehearsals.

5. Producer agrees to pay Actor's assistant one hundred ($100) dollars a week as reimbursement for cab fare.

6. Producer agrees to offer Actor a nonaccountable allowance of four thousand ($4,000) dollars to cover the expense of her two children and daughter-in-law flying into New York and returning to California over the Christmas holidays, and to pay for their staying in a good, but not necessarily deluxe, midtown hotel while they are here.

7. Upon presentation of an actual bill from _____ Kennels, Producer agrees to reimburse either Actor, or the kennel, at Actor's election, for the cost of kenneling Actor's dog for the rehearsal period, such cost not to exceed _____.

8. Producer agrees to provide Actor with a vocal coach prior to the start of rehearsals. Actor hereby acknowledges that such vocal work has already commenced, and approves _____ as the vocal coach.

Very truly yours,
BROADWAY ENTITY

_____

General Manager

NOTE: *This side letter, which does not go to the union, contains negotiated provisions that are not covered in the Equity agreement and, therefore, are not under their jurisdiction. All of the above items are terms I have actually agreed to for a variety of star actors.*

6

Sample Star Director Contract Rider

On Broadway, a director's contract is subject to the jurisdiction of the Stage Directors and Choreographers Society (SDC). In a standard contract, a director receives a fee and an advance (against royalties); at the time of writing, the SDC minimum fee for a director of a play is $33,245, and the minimum advance is $25,710, for a combined total of $58,955. The SDC required minimum royalty for a director of a play is 1.5 percent. The contract rider that follows is for a star director, so the negotiated financial terms are considerably above these minimums. Because the amount of the fee is above minimum, the union has allowed the director to receive a smaller than minimum advance; combined, both are still well above the current minimum fee and advance. Note, too, the special provisions for concerns such as creative approvals, travel and living expenses, billing, house seats, opening night seats and party passes, right of first refusal to direct future productions, response time for acceptance or declination to direct future productions, an assistant, expenses, and insurance. Many of the issues are similar to those just reviewed in our star actor's contract, while some are unique to the services a director provides.

AGREEMENT ("Agreement") made as of this _____ th day of
_____ 20 ___ by and between _____ ("Director"), c/o
_____ Agency, _____ New York, NY
100__, Attn: _____, and _____ ("Producer"),
c/o _____ New York, NY
100__ attn: _____, in connection with the play entitled
"_____" ("Play") by _____
("Author").

The parties do hereby agree as follows:

1. **ENGAGEMENT.** Producer hereby engages Director to direct the Play,
and Director hereby accepts such engagement upon all the terms and conditions herein set forth.

2. **TERM OF EXCLUSIVE ENGAGEMENT.** Director's nonexclusive
services shall commence with the execution of this Agreement and shall
continue until the commencement of rehearsals of the Play, currently
scheduled for on or about _____, previewing on or about
_____ in New York City, with an Official Press Opening in
New York City on or about _____. Director shall provide
first-priority services, with no outside commitment permitted to interfere
with Director's full and timely completion of Director's services on the
Play, for the period from the commencement of rehearsals up through the
Official Press Opening. Producer shall provide Director with fifteen (15)
days notice of any change in the date of the first rehearsal. Should the
proposed schedule hereinabove change by no more than two (2) weeks,
Director shall be obligated to provide service hereunder. For a delay of
more than two (2) weeks, Director will have the option of electing whether
or not Director will provide service. Notice of Director's acceptance shall
be governed by the terms in paragraph 25, following.

NOTE: *Unlike an actor, whose services normally begin on the first day of
rehearsal, a director's services begin long before then and entail playing the
dominant role, with the author and producer having approval, in all matters artistic—casting, selecting designers, consulting with the set designer
to develop the scenic design of the play, viewing prospective theaters to
determine their suitability, working with the author (if it is a new play) on*

script changes, etc. For these preproduction duties, the director's services are nonexclusive. For the intense, consecutive period beginning with the start of rehearsals and continuing through opening night, however, it is imperative that the director's services to the show be exclusive.

3. NATURE OF SERVICES. Director shall render all services customarily rendered by the director of a Broadway production, including supervising and conducting rehearsals, attending and supervising all New York previews and the official New York City opening of the Play. Director shall also attend conferences, consult with the Producer, and make suggestions with regard to casting and other production aspects.

4. APPROVALS. Director shall have prior reasonable approval with Author and Producer of the following elements of all companies of the Play directed by him hereunder, not to be unreasonably delayed: cast, understudies, stage manager, theater, scenic, costume, lighting and sound designers, musical and sound effects to be used for the Play, Composer and/or Musical Director (if any), and all replacements and substitutes thereof, as well as prior reasonable approval of any replacement director of a production Director is entitled to, and elects not to, direct only where Director's original direction is being substantially replicated. Director's failure to communicate disapproval of any of the foregoing elements within three (3) business days after Director's receipt of Producer's request for approval (specifically citing the reply deadline) or seventy-two (72) hours in the case where a response is clearly identified as being extremely time sensitive shall be deemed approval.

Director hereby approves _____ as the cast, _____ as Set Designer, _____ as Costume Designer, _____ as Lighting Designer, _____ as Sound Designer, _____ as the composer of Original Music, _____ as production stage manager, and the _____ Theater.

NOTE: As remarked above, in his role as captain of all things artistic, the director is assured approval, with the author and producer, of all the positions enumerated above and others if required. If any personnel have already been decided on at the time of the director's hiring, this is where the specific names of those individuals should be indicated.

5. **CHANGES IN STAGING.** Director agrees to give due consideration to any reasonable requests made by the Producer for changes in staging or performances of any company of the Play directed by Director hereunder, but no changes shall be made in the staging or performance of any such company without Director's and Producer's prior consent.

NOTE: *The director's work is protected. No changes can be made to the direction without the director* and *producer's prior consent.*

6. **SERVICES AFTER OPENING.** After the Opening of the Play in New York City, Director, subject to prior professional commitments, will check performances of the Play from time to time and direct rehearsals and cast replacements to the extent reasonably necessary to maintain the quality of the Play without additional compensation therefore, but his failure to do so shall not be deemed a breach of this Agreement.

NOTE: *Here is another major difference between the duties of a director and those of an actor—an actor provides services during the term of his employment only, but a director is responsible for maintaining the artistic integrity of the show for the entirety of its run. That is part of the reason a director gets an ongoing royalty. And it is therefore in the director's best interest to maintain the show as best as possible—so it will continue to run, and the director will continue to receive his or her royalty!*

7. **TRAVEL AND LIVING EXPENSES.** At any time when Director is required by Producer to be more than ninety (90) miles outside of his residence in New York City in connection with rehearsals or performances of any production of the Play hereunder, Producer agrees to provide him with a mutually acceptable one-bedroom apartment or a first-class hotel (inclusive of applicable taxes and work-related telephone calls only, but exclusive of personal telephone usage, room service, and all other charges), at his election, plus a per diem of one hundred ($100.00) dollars (one hundred (£100) pounds in London) and shall provide Director with round-trip regular business class airfare between New York City and the city where

the Director's presence is required. In addition to the foregoing, when Director's presence is required for casting, rehearsals, or performances in Los Angeles (or any other such location where the use of an automobile is mutually agreed to be reasonably necessary for local transport), Director shall be reimbursed for the cost of a self-drive rental car, including minimum insurance, work-related fuel, parking, and tolls.

NOTE: *Fairly similar to the language in the star actor's contract, although, here, if a car is needed, the director normally is provided with a rental car and drives it himself, while a star actor will be provided with a car and driver. Also, being a less publicly recognizable celebrity than a star actor, a director is more likely to agree to fly business class.*

8. BILLING AND PUBLICITY. In all paid advertising, house boards, and programs under the Producer's control or authority, the Director shall be given credit in substantially the following manner:

Directed by

_____

Only the Producer, the author, and stars billed above the title shall be entitled to receive credit in a size as large as the credit accorded to Director. Only the name of the theater and stars billed above the title shall be entitled to receive credit in a size larger than the credit accorded to Director. Except for "movie-style billing" or "run-on billing," Director's credit shall be on a line by itself and shall be the last credit afforded any creative personnel engaged for the production, in a type size not less than fifty (50%) percent of the size of the largest type size used for the title in the same applicable billing item, or fifty (50%) percent of the size of the credit for any stars billed above the title, whichever is larger.

In the event a logo title is utilized, Director's credit shall not be less than 33.33% of the size of the logo title. Notwithstanding the foregoing, Producer shall in no event have any obligation to give Director credit in "teaser" lists, awards, congratulatory, nomination, or institutional advertisements (except that if within such advertisement the Play is being awarded or congratulated or nominated, then billing is required for the Director) and critics quotes.

With respect to quote ads, the Director shall either be given a quote or shall be billed. Producer shall have no obligation to bill Director in directory or daily informational advertisements (except "ABC ads," where Director shall receive credit), heralds, and seasonal listings, and/or ticket price scales, and tickets. Director shall not be billed on underslings or banners in which only the title appears. Director shall not be required to be billed on the marquee if only the title, artwork title, and/or logo of the Play, the name(s) of Producer and/or the theater, and the name(s) and/or image(s) of the star(s) are billed. In the event that Director is not billed on the marquee, Producer will utilize an undersling to bill Director.

Wherever credits are accorded in connection with the Play in a so-called "billing box" pursuant to which Director is entitled to credit, the size of Director's credit in said "billing box" shall be equal to all other persons being billed in such billing box. Where credit is given in a so-called billing box, no person, firm, or entity may receive credit outside of a billing box except the logo of the Producer, if applicable, the name of the theater, the artwork title and/or logo title of the Play. If any such credit is used for any other person, firm, or entity outside of such billing box, Director's credit shall appear outside of such billing box in proportion to the title pursuant to this paragraph 8.

Producer shall be entitled to utilize "movie-style billing" or "run-on billing," provided that all persons receiving credit shall be billed on the same basis, in the same size and typeface. Where credit is given on such "movie-style billing" basis, the size of the credit given to all persons receiving credit shall be equal to the size of the credit accorded to the nonartwork title of the Play. Where movie-style billing is utilized, no person, firm, or entity may receive credit in any manner other than movie-style billing except the logo of the Producer, if any, the name of the theater, the artwork title and/or logo of the Play, and stars billed above the title.

Notwithstanding the provision of this paragraph 8, Director agrees that with respect to advertisements where Director's name appears in a "critic's quote" Producer's obligation, if any, to accord Director credit shall be deemed to have been satisfied in all regards provided that all other credits other than stars are found only in critic's quotes in such advertisements.

Any casual or inadvertent failure to comply with the provisions of this paragraph shall not constitute a default under the terms of this Agreement, provided Producer shall be obligated to cure prospectively such failure with reasonable dispatch after written notice from Director or Director's agent.

Director shall have approval of his biography and any photographic likeness, if used, appearing in programs or other materials under the Producer's reasonable control.

Subject to Director's professional availability, Director agrees to cooperate fully with Producer in publicizing the Play, subject to his right to approve all publicity work he does so long as in aggregate he does a reasonable and customary amount of such work. For all such work Director does at Producer's request to publicize the Play, Director shall be reimbursed for all out-of-pocket expenses, not to exceed $100 without Producer's prior written approval, and car service shall be provided for any interviews or appearances requested of Director by Producer.

NOTE: These are all fairly standard terms for a prominent director. As with star actors, a lot of ego is invested in where, how, and when a director receives billing. Note how there are negotiated stipulations for the size of the director's billing relative to the size of the play's title that cover a broad range of advertising options—regular title, logo artwork title, appearing within a billing box, as part of movie-style (continuous, run-on) billing, etc.

9. **COMPENSATION.** In full compensation for Director's services as Director of the Broadway production of the Play Director shall receive the following:

(a) A Fee in the amount of sixty thousand ($60,000) dollars, and an Advance in the amount of ten thousand ($10,000) dollars, for a combined total of seventy thousand ($70,000) dollars, payable seventeen thousand five hundred ($17,500) dollars upon execution of this Agreement, seventeen thousand five hundred ($17,500) dollars on the first day of the first week of rehearsal, seventeen thousand five hundred ($17,500) dollars on the first day of the second week of rehearsal, and the balance of seventeen thousand five hundred ($17,500) dollars payable on the first day of the third week of rehearsal, each of the foregoing payments being nonreturnable.

(b) Royalty based on Gross:

(i) Commencing with the first paid public performance of the Play, Director shall receive a royalty of 3% of "Gross Weekly Box Office Receipts" ("GWBOR," as defined below) or, in losing weeks, a minimum weekly guarantee ("MWG") of $3,000, prorated on the basis of an eight-performance week. The royalty will increase to 4% of GWBOR at 110% of Recoupment (as defined below), and Director's MWG will increase to $4,000, prorated on the basis of an eight-performance week, at that time as well. Only amounts in excess of the MWG are applicable against the Advance.

(ii) In any week in which the GWBOR are between 100% and 110% of Weekly Breakeven (the so-called "Grey Zone" referenced in Article IV(B)(2(a)(i) of the SDC Agreement), Director shall receive, in lieu of the percentage royalty in 9(b)(i) above, a MWG of $3,000, plus 7.5 % of weekly Net Operating Profits ("NOP," as defined below), if any, which shall not exceed in the aggregate 3% of GWBOR until 110% of Recoupment, and 4% of GWBOR above 110% of Recoupment. The foregoing shall only apply in the event that the royalties to the Author and all other percentage royalty recipients are calculated on the basis of the Grey Zone. Sums payable under the Grey Zone over the minimum guarantee shall be credited against the advance.

(c) Alternative royalty based on Net: If Producer elects to compensate Author, Producer and all other percentage royalty recipients based on weekly net operating profit ("NOP," as defined below), Company shall be entitled to receive a MWG of $3,000 payable weekly and prorated on the basis of an eight-performance week against 7.5% of any weekly NOP, rising to 10% at 110% of recoupment. Only amounts in excess of Director's MWG shall be applicable against the Advance.

"Full Performance Week," "Weekly Profits," "Gross Weekly Box Office Receipts," weekly "Net Operating Profits," and "Weekly Breakeven" shall be defined per the Dramatists Guild Approved Production Contract for Plays, and in any event shall be on a favored nations basis with all royalty participants. "Net Profits" shall not be subject to any right of recall or accumulation for additional companies.

With respect to any so-called "guaranteed" or "fixed fee" bookings, Director's royalties shall be computed on the "Company Share" in lieu of gross weekly box office receipts, if the Author's royalties, Producer's management fee, and the participation of all other percentage royalty recipients including the Producer (excluding theatre(s) and star(s) if they shall be percentage royalty participants) are so computed. The term "Company Share" shall be deemed to include all receipts derived by Producer from such guaranteed or fixed-fee bookings (including but not limited to fixed fees, guarantees, and any Producer's share of box office receipts and any payments directly to a star made by any third party) after the deduction therefrom of deductions permitted under the Dramatists Guild's APC definition of gross weekly box office receipts and any booking fee charged by any tour booking agents.

NOTE: Again, this is for a star director. The total amount of the fee and advance is about 20% above the SDC minimum. The agent initially wanted his client to receive a fee of $70,000 and no advance, but I was able to negotiate a fee of $60,000 plus an advance of $10,000. The advance is against earned royalties, which are operating expenses, so this lower fee figure helps to reduce production expenses. The agent also wanted his client to initially receive a percentage royalty of 4 percent, but I was able to defer 1 percent of that until not just recoupment, but 110 percent of recoupment, allowing the investors a little breathing room after recoupment (remember, at that point they still haven't received 100 percent of their capital contribution back, just the majority portion of it which constitutes the production expenses) before the weekly operating expenses increase. There are also negotiated terms here for a minimum weekly guarantee in losing weeks, an option for reduced payments in the "Grey Zone," when the gross is between breakeven and 110 percent of breakeven, and an alternative, at the producer's election, to change the calculation of the director's royalty from being based on gross (weekly box office receipts) to being based on weekly net (operating profits).

10. **HOUSE SEATS.** For all productions of the Play presented hereunder within Producer's control, lease, or license, Director or his designee shall be entitled to purchase at regular box office prices two (2) adjacent pair of center orchestra seats in rows 4 through 12 (for theater party, press, or Tony-voter performances for which the center orchestra is substantially sold out, one (1) pair in such location,) for each evening and matinee performance (including previews) of the Play. Per Producer's contract with

the theater, such tickets shall be held on a 96-hour release basis and shall be held in the Producer's office for Director's use. Producer agrees to keep such books and records as may be required to comply with the rules and regulations of the attorney general of the State of New York or any other governmental agency having jurisdiction.

NOTE: *Pretty standard and comparable to what a star actor receives.*

11. **OFFICIAL PRESS OPENING.** For the Official Press Opening Night performance of the Broadway Production, Director shall be entitled to receive, at no charge, five (5) pairs of seats, three (3) pairs in the center orchestra in rows 4 through 12, and two (2) pairs on best available orchestra side aisles and five (5) pairs of tickets to the opening night party. Director shall be entitled to purchase additional pairs of orchestra seats and tickets to the opening night party as needed. Director shall have suffi-cient reserved tables at the opening night party to accommodate his guests.

NOTE: *Again, pretty standard. Star actors and directors will want assurance that their guests will have a reserved place to sit at the opening night party.*

12. **ASSISTANT.** Producer shall provide Director with a mutually approved assistant at a salary or fee to be approved by Producer for the period from first rehearsal through the official opening of the Play in New York City, and for all additional companies which he elects to direct hereunder.

NOTE: *Directors will always need an assistant, if for nothing else then to act as a secretary to take down their notes during rehearsals and run-throughs. The implication here is that the director did not have someone in mind to work with him, which means the GM can come up with a young, eager, bright gofer, happy to get this experience for a modest weekly stipend.*

13. **EXPENSES.** Producer agrees to reimburse Director within seven (7) days of submission of organized, itemized receipts and/or supporting docu-mentation for all usual and customary expenses incurred in connection with his services hereunder, including but not limited to long-distance telephone and facsimile transmission charges, photocopies, local transportation to

and from meetings/auditions, etc. Director agrees to obtain prior approval from Producer's office for any expense in excess of $100.

NOTE: It is not by chance that the word "organized" appears here. There is nothing more frustrating, and unacceptable, than being handed an envelope crammed with loose, unorganized receipts. Receipts should be numbered, and they should be itemized, identified, and totaled on a legible cover sheet. And then the company manager (or an assistant or intern) should review each and every one, checking the amount on the cover sheet against the amount on the receipt and making sure there have not been any errors in totaling the receipts.

14. **AUDIOVISUAL RECORDING.** Producer shall not permit filming, televising, or other reproduction or transmission of any complete or partial performance of the Play directed by Director without first negotiating and executing a written agreement with Director in respect thereof, unless such filming or taping falls under the approved Actors' Equity Association Media Promotion and Publicity and Other Recording and Broadcast Provisions, the sole uses of which are for promotional or publicity purposes. Notwithstanding the foregoing, Producer shall have the right to authorize one or more radio and/or television presentations and/or commercials using excerpts of the Play as directed by Director (each such presentation and/or commercial not to exceed five (5) minutes in length) for the sole purpose of advertising and publicizing the Play, including, without limitation, showing on award programs such as the Antoinette Perry Award program, provided that neither Producer nor any person or entity affiliated with Producer will receive any monetary compensation or other consideration or profit (other than reimbursement of customary, direct out-of-pocket expenses of Producer relating to such production), directly or indirectly, for authorizing any such radio or television presentation.

NOTE: This is boilerplate.

15. **INSURANCE.** In the event Producer chooses to purchase Errors and Omission insurance for any company of the Play, Producer will use best efforts to have the Director named as an additional insured with respect

to such insurance. In the event the addition of the Director as an additional insured increases the cost of the insurance, and Director elects to be covered in such cases, Director shall remit the cost of the increase to the Producer.

Producer hereby agrees to cause Director to be named as an additional insured on all liability insurance policies carried by Producer, and Producer agrees to deliver to Director an irrevocable policy or certificate therefore.

NOTE: It is standard to issue the director a certificate naming him as an additional insured on the show's liability insurance policy. The theater will want this, as will stars, the lead producer(s), all coproducers receiving above the title billing, the author, the designers, the GM, the technical supervisor, and the rental equipment shops. And if someone has a loan-out company, then he will want certificates both for him as an individual and for his company! It is not unusual these days to request fifty additional insured certificates from the show's insurance broker. The GM has to keep track of everyone who requires one and make sure the certificates are issued.

16. **ADDITIONAL COMPANIES.** (a) Provided that Director is not in material breach of any term of this Agreement and is credited as Director of the Play as of the Official Press Opening in New York City, and if any one or more companies or stage productions of the Play is produced anywhere in the United States under the Producer's control, lease, license, or assignment, Director shall be given the right of first refusal to direct same for terms no less favorable than the terms of this Agreement for any first-class productions and, as stated below, for any non-first-class productions. If the production is a foreign production, then Director shall be given the right of first refusal to direct same at terms and conditions to be negotiated in good faith and commensurate for a director of his stature in that other territory. The above notwithstanding, for any first-class US productions, Director shall receive the same terms and conditions of this Agreement provided he is present for at least one-half of the rehearsals. If Director is present for at least 25% of the rehearsals but less than 50%, he shall receive no less than 50% of the negotiated fee in paragraph 9(a) hereinabove and 75% of the minimum royalties in paragraph 9(b) hereinabove and 100% of the pension and health payments due therefore. If Director is

present for less than 25% of the rehearsals, he shall not receive any fee or pension and health payments in respect to such company, but will receive no less than 50% of the minimum royalties in paragraph 9(b) hereinabove.

(b) In the case of a non-first-class production, if Director directs any such additional company, Producer shall pay or cause to be paid to Director the following with respect to each such additional company which Director directs:

(i) A fee and advance equal to one hundred and forty percent (140%) of the minimum fee and advance required pursuant to the applicable SDC collective bargaining agreement; plus

(ii) A royalty in an amount equal to four percent (4%) of GWBOR. Notwithstanding the foregoing, both Producer and Director agree that, provided all other royalty holders agree, should Producer wish to activate a Royalty Pool option at a future time, both parties shall negotiate the terms of said Royalty Pool in good faith.

(c) If Director shall decline to direct any such additional production referred to in the preceding paragraph, Producer shall, nevertheless, pay or cause to be paid to Director a royalty, payable weekly, equal to the royalty set forth in paragraph 9(b) herein less the royalty payable to the new director, but reducible only to a floor of 50% of Director's royalty as set forth in paragraph 9 (b) hereinabove. This royalty shall be subject to 9(c), if applicable, but in no event shall Director receive any fee or advance.

(d) If Director shall decline to direct any such additional production referred to in the preceding paragraph, Director shall receive the following credit in all programs and wherever the subsequent director receives credit in a size one hundred percent (100%) of the size of the credit accorded to the subsequent director, but not less than fifty percent (50%) of the title:

"Originally directed on Broadway by _____"

(e) Producer shall give Director not less than sixty (60) days prior written notice of each such additional production, thirty (30) days in the event of a transfer from one theater to another, which notice shall specify the rehearsal commencement date and place of rehearsal as contemplated. Within ten (10) business days after receipt of such notice, Director shall notify Producer whether or not he elects to direct such production. Director's failure to give Producer such notice shall be deemed a declination and, in such event, Director's right of election with respect to the particular production shall forthwith terminate and Producer shall be free to employ another director for such company. Any declination does not affect Director's right of first refusal on any subsequent productions.

(f) In the event that the Play is presented initially or is transferred or presented subsequent to the initial production in the United States or Canada as a first-class production or a prior production is upgraded under Producer's whole or partial management or control or by assignment, lease, or license or under authorization by Producer during the term of its production rights, Director shall have the exclusive irrevocable option to direct same upon the same terms and conditions herein, and any previous unrecouped fee and/or advance payments shall be applied toward the sum of the upgraded fee and/or advance. If Director shall decline to direct such production of the Play, paragraph 16(c) shall apply.

NOTE: *You can see how complicated it is to prenegotiate the director's right of first refusal to direct the play in different territories and in different classes of production. Note that in the United States, for other first-class productions, the director's terms will be no less favorable than the terms stated in this contract. However, in a foreign production, the director shall be given the right of first refusal to direct the play for terms and conditions to be negotiated in good faith and commensurate for a director of his stature in that other territory. I learned this lesson the hard way. I began incorporating this language into all my subsequent director contracts whenever we wanted to find an English coproducer for a successful Broadway show that utilized a star American director with an over-scale deal. It turned out that terms like the ones granted here are considerably above market rate for a star director in London, and our British partner couldn't make the numbers attractive to investors in the West End. In the end, we had to give up our own vested right to license the play in the British Isles and return this right to the author, in exchange for receiving a percentage of the*

author's subsidiary income from this production. Thus, a London produc-
tion would no longer be under the US producer's control, lease, license, or
assignment; instead, it would be under direct license from the author. This
meant the London producer would be unencumbered by any rights of first
refusal or prenegotiated financial deals we had made for Broadway.

17. REMITTANCE OF PAYMENTS.

All payments to Director shall be made in the name of
_____ c/o _____ Agency, and mailed
to _____, _____, New York, NY
100___, attn: _____.

Royalties payable to Director hereunder will be payable within seven
(7) days after the week in which earned. The above notwithstanding, with
respect to productions more than 500 miles from New York City, royalties
shall be paid within fourteen (14) days, and with respect to productions in
the Additional or Supplemental Territories, within twenty-one (21) days,
following the end of each performance week.

If such payments are delayed through no fault of Producer, then such
delay shall not constitute a breach of this Agreement.

All percentage payments shall be accompanied by box office and weekly
profit and loss statements in customary form indicating receipts and costs
for performances given during such week. Said statements shall be signed
by the Producer or its duly authorized representative and the treasurer of
the theatre.

There shall be no waivers, reductions or deferrals of Director's royalties
hereunder, without Director's express written consent. All fees, advances,
minimums, and weekly royalties hereunder shall be paid in US dollars,
without deduction for currency exchange, bank charges, or transfer fees,
in accordance with the attached banking instructions.

NOTE: All pretty standard. Note that royalty recipients expect to see cop-
ies of box office statements that prove what the week's gross was, as well
as weekly accounting statements that show if the week ended in profit or
loss. Throw in an individualized cover sheet, and a copy of all of the above
to SDC, and that adds up to a lot of back-up that must accompany every
royalty check each week.

18. EXAMINATION OF BOOKS AND RECORDS. Director or his designee shall have the right, at reasonable business hours and for a reasonable number of times, to examine the books and records of Producer pertaining to the Play and the exploitation of any rights therein for the purpose of verifying any statements and/or ascertaining any amounts which may be due Director hereunder. Director shall have the right to make extracts from such books and records, or copies thereof, and/or cause an audit to be made thereof, all at Director's sole expense. Any such inspection shall take place at the location where such books and records are regularly kept, at a time to be mutually determined by Producer and Director.

Notwithstanding the foregoing, should any such audit reveal an underpayment to the Director of greater than ten percent (10%), the Producer shall bear the full expense of the audit.

NOTE: Boilerplate. An audit of the show's books and records, all kept in the GM's office, is a major disruption to the ongoing process of managing a major Broadway show. Only once in thirty years of working in the professional theater have I seen an audit requested, and it didn't yield any different results than what the show had previously reported.

19. REPRESENTATIONS AND WARRANTIES: INDEMNIFICATION. (a) Director represents, warrants, and agrees: that he has the right to enter into this Agreement, to grant the rights stated herein, and to furnish the services stated herein; that Director is not subject to any obligations or disability which will prevent or interfere with the due performance of all the covenants and conditions to be performed by him hereunder; that he has not made, nor will he make, any grant or assignment which will conflict with or impair the complete enjoyment of the rights and privilege granted hereunder; and that the direction created by Director will be wholly original with him and will not infringe upon or violate the copyright, contract right, or personal right of any other party whatsoever.

(b) To the extent permitted by the SDC agreement, Director agrees to indemnify and hold harmless Producer, its successor, licensees, and assigns from and against any and all damages, liabilities, and/or expenses (including, without limitation, reasonable outside attorney's fees) incurred by Producer or such parties claiming through Producer, resulting from any breach (as determined by a final nonappealable judgment or decree or by a settlement agreed in writing by Director) of any representation, warranty, or agreement made by Director in this agreement.

(c) Producer agrees to indemnify and hold harmless Director and his loan-out company, if applicable, its successor, licensees, and assigns from and against any and all damages, liabilities, and/or expenses (including, without limitation, reasonable outside attorney's fees) incurred by Director or such parties claiming through Director, resulting from any breach of any representation, warranty, or agreement made by Producer in this agreement or otherwise arising in connection with this Agreement, or Producer's development or production of the Play (except to the extent caused by Director's express indemnity set forth in paragraph 19 (b)).

NOTE: *The representations, warranties, and indemnifications are recipro-cal—both sides extend them to the other. Note, too, that the director is stating that he has no (undisclosed) disability that would prevent or inter-fere with his providing his services to the show.*

20. **OWNERSHIP OF DIRECTOR'S CONTRIBUTIONS.** All rights in and to the direction conceived by Director in the course of the rendition of his services hereunder shall be, upon its creation and shall remain, as between Producer and Director, Director's sole and exclusive property, it being understood, however, that Producer shall have a perpetual and irrev-ocable license to use such direction in any production of the Play for which Director is offered the option to direct (provided Director is ready, willing, and able to direct) and receives the compensation pursuant to the terms of this Agreement. Producer shall not authorize the publication in any form of the stage directions of the Director without his written consent.

NOTE: *A very important concept: the direction belongs to (is the sole and exclusive property of) the director, but the producer, as long as he or she compensates the director for its use, has a perpetual and irrevo-cable license to use that direction. This language protects the director's contribution—the look and feel of a production as embodied in its overall concept, staging, casting, performances, and design—from ever being used without the director being compensated for it. Either the director will be paid to literally direct future productions or tours that are replicas of the original Broadway production, or, if he or she is not available, the director will be compensated when someone else, normally with his or her right of approval, is hired to recreate the director's original work.*

21. WAIVER. No waiver by either of the parties hereto or any failure by the other party to keep or perform any covenant or condition of this Agreement shall be deemed to be a waiver of any preceding or succeeding breach of the same, or any other covenant or condition.

NOTE: Boilerplate.

22. ASSIGNMENT OR LICENSE.
(a) The Producer may assign this Agreement and may license or assign any of the rights granted hereunder, providing, however, that the assignment of the right to produce the Play in New York City may only be made to a limited partnership, joint venture, corporation, or other entity in which Producer is a general partner, joint venturer, or has a majority or controlling interest (or a corporation controlled by him).

For all other productions outside of New York City, Producer may assign this Agreement and may license any of the rights granted hereunder without Director's approval so long as Producer remains the controlling general partner or venturer.

In the event Producer assigns this Agreement and licenses any of the rights granted hereunder to a nonunion producing entity, in which Producer cannot remain the controlling general partner or venturer, Director hereby preapproves the following entities: _____.

Director shall not have the right to assign this Agreement except to an entity/company controlled by Director.

 (b) If the Producer either assigns or licenses to a third party the right to produce the Play, Producer shall provide in the agreement therefore that such assignee or licensee shall assume all the obligations to the Director set forth herein with respect to its production of the Play, and Producer shall continue to have liability if such assignee or licensee fails to duly perform any such obligation, and Director shall look solely to the Producer for such performance and for any remedy for default by such assignee or licensee.

NOTE: Boilerplate.

23. **NOTICES.** Any notice required or desired to be given hereunder shall be sent by registered or certified mail, return receipt requested, or telegraph or cable addressed to the parties at their respective addresses given herein, or by delivering same personally to the parties at the addresses first set forth herein. Any party may designate a different address by notice so given.

Copies of all such notices to the Producer shall be sent to:

_____(GM office)

c/o_____

New York, NY 100__

Attn: _____

cc: (show attorney)

_____

_____

_____

Cc: (producer)

_____

_____

_____

To the Director:

_____

c/o _____

_____

New York, NY 100___

Attn: _____

NOTE: Boilerplate.

24. ABANDONMENT, POSTPONEMENT, AND CLOSING OF THE
RUN OF THE PLAY. Producer shall have the right at any time to abandon or postpone the production of the Play. In the event the Producer exercises such right, Director shall retain all monies theretofore paid to him, shall promptly receive any compensation in which he has vested prior to the date of abandonment that may be owed him, as per paragraph 9 (a), and Producer shall have no further obligation to Director hereunder. If Producer shall reschedule rehearsals that have been abandoned or postponed, Producer shall use all reasonable efforts to give Director not less than forty-five (45) days prior written notice specifying the new rehearsal commencement date, in the case of each such change or postponement. Director shall have a period of ten (10) days after receipt of such notice within which to give Producer notice as to whether Director is available. Director shall be deemed available if the new noticed rehearsal period is set to begin within two (2) weeks of the schedule outlined in paragraph 2, above. If Director is available, Director shall furnish his services hereunder for the same terms agreed to herein, and Producer shall then have a credit in the amount of all monies theretofore paid to Director with respect to such company.

For the purpose of clarity, should the current schedule proposed in paragraph 2 above change by no more than two (2) weeks for any reason other than force majeure (as described in paragraph 25, below), Director shall be obligated to provide service hereunder. For a postponement of more than two (2) weeks, Director will have the election of deciding whether or not Director will provide service.

If Director is not available, Director shall so notify Producer and shall furnish, at Producer's request, specifics as to Director's prior commitments. Declination because of unavailability shall not affect Director's right to receive such option with respect to any further rescheduling if, at that time, another director shall not have been engaged.

The Producer shall have the right to close the run of the Play at any time he desires.

NOTE: *Complicated provisions, trying to foresee every conceivable situation involving the abandonment, postponement, and closing of the play, as well as predetermining the director's rights and/or obligations in each situation.*

25. **FORCE MAJEURE.** If Producer shall be prevented from producing any production of the Play within any applicable time period set forth herein, or if any production produced hereunder shall be interrupted, due to fire, strikes, labor disputes, government or court order, war, act of terrorism, or civil commotion or any other cause beyond the Producer's control, such prevention or interruption shall not be deemed a breach of this agreement and the applicable time periods set forth herein shall be extended for the actual number of days of such prevention or interruption not to exceed 120 days.

Should any of the hereinabove referenced forms of force majeur persist for greater than six (6) months, Director shall have the right to terminate this agreement.

NOTE: After 9/11, an act of terrorism had to be added to this list of what constitutes force majeure.

26. **NO INJUNCTION.** In the event of a breach of this agreement by the Producer, Director's remedy shall be limited to money damages; in no event shall he be entitled to seek or obtain injunctive relief (note: a court order requiring a person to do, or ease doing, a specific action); and any arbitrator appointed under this agreement shall be bound by this provision.

NOTE: Boilerplate.

27. **ARBITRATION.** Any controversy or claim arising out of or relating to this Agreement, or the breach thereof, shall be settled by expeditious arbitration in New York City in accordance with the rules of the American Arbitration Association, and the Stage Directors and Choreographers Society shall be a party to such arbitration. Such arbitration shall be settled by a single arbitrator and judgment upon the award rendered by said arbitrator may be entered in the highest court of the forum, State or Federal, having jurisdiction thereof. The arbitrator is authorized to assess the defaulting party for the reasonable counsel fees and expenses incurred by the nondefaulting party in connection with the arbitration proceeding.

NOTE: *Boilerplate, although important to include that the location of the arbitration is in New York City and that it can be resolved by a single arbitrator.*

28. THIS AGREEMENT.

(a) Shall be binding upon and inure to the benefit of the parties hereto and their respective heirs, executors, administrators, and assigns;

(b) Shall be construed and enforced in accordance with the laws of the State of New York, regardless of the actual place of execution, and shall be operative throughout the world;

(c) Shall constitute the entire understanding between the parties and may not be modified or amended except in writing signed by each of the parties hereto.

(d) Shall incorporate the Collective Bargaining Agreement between the Stage Directors and Choreographers Society and The Broadway League effective September 1, 2015, and as amended, the terms and conditions of which shall apply with respect to all additional first-class companies hereunder. Except to the extent the terms and conditions of this Rider and/ or any other applicable collectively bargained agreement—i.e. Canadian Equity, SOLT, etc.—are more favorable to the Director than the terms and conditions of the SDC-Broadway Agreement, in the event of a conflict, the SDC-Broadway Agreement shall control.

NOTE: *Boilerplate. In (d), all the terms and conditions of the current SDC contract are folded into this rider. They are a given; this rider addresses issues and terms not covered by that agreement.*

AGENCY. Director hereby irrevocably appoints _____ Agency ("Agent") as Director's sole and exclusive agent with respect to all income to be received by Director hereunder. In consideration of the services rendered by Agent hereunder and in the future, Director authorizes Producer to deduct and pay Agent ten percent (10%) of the gross compensation paid to Director hereunder and derived from future sale or licensing rights in Director's direction.

NOTE: *Boilerplate. This clause authorizes the GM's office to deduct 10 percent of the director's compensation and forward it directly to the agent* *on the director's behalf. This is a service to the director and means no one else has to keep track of his or her earnings, calculate and deduct 10 percent, provide copies of box office statements and weekly profit and loss statements as back-up, and send it all to the agent.*

IN WITNESS WHEREOF, the parties have hereunto set their hands and seals the day and year first written above.

_____ L.P.

By: _____   By: _____

_____   _____, General Manager

7

Sample Star Designer Contract Rider

Design contracts on Broadway are subject to the jurisdiction of United Scenic Artists (USA), Local 829. The following contract rider is for a play, the designer has his own corporate loan-out company that provides his services, and the design falls under the USA set classification of Dramatic Single Set. (Plays have different negotiated rates than musicals, and both categories have three subclassifications—for a single set, a multiset, and a unit set with phases—each with its own proscribed minimum fee and advance). As a point of reference for this contract rider, the current (at time of writing) USA minimums for a Dramatic Single Set are a fee of $9,217 and an advance of $2,311, for a combined total of $11,528. The current USA minimum flat royalty, referred to as an **additional weekly compensation (AWC)**, for this design category, prerecoupment, is $332.97.

Having reviewed a number of different contract riders by now, you should begin to see certain similarities in the kinds of issues that they cover—many clauses are standard boilerplate (indemnification, breach and cure, arbitration, right to audit, insurance) while others are individual and negotiable (compensation, billing, house seats, opening night tickets, number of assistant weeks).

RIDER TO UNITED SCENIC ARTISTS STANDARD SCENIC DESIGN CONTRACT DATED _____ BETWEEN _____ DESIGN LTD F/S/O _____ (DESIGNER) AND _____ BROADWAY LLC (PRODUCER) WITH RESPECT TO THE PRODUCTION OF "_____" (PLAY) AT THE _____ THEATER IN NEW YORK CITY.

Wherever and whenever the provisions of this Rider differ from or conflict with the printed portion of this contract, the provisions of this Rider shall control.

1. **FEE.** A stated fee of $20,000, payable as follows: One-fourth (1/4) upon signing, one-fourth (1/4) when painting or construction of the set commences in the shop, one-fourth (1/4) on the first paid public performance, and one-fourth (1/4) on or before the official opening in New York City. There shall be no advance.

NOTE: *Because the fee is more than double the current USA minimum for this design category, no advance is required.*

2. **ROYALTY.** Commencing with the first paid public performance, and through the week in which 110% recoupment of production costs occurs, a minimum guarantee (prorated on the basis of an eight (8) performance week) of $1,000/wk, against a fixed AWC based on gross weekly box office receipts as follows:

$0	to	$300,000	$1,000
$300,001	to	$350,000	$1,625
$350,001	to	$400,000	$1,875
$400,001	to	$450,000	$2,125
$450,001	to	$500,000	$2,375
$500,001	to	$550,000	$2,625
$550,001	to	$600,000	$2,875
$600,001	to	$650,000	$3,125
$650,001	to	$700,000	$3,375
$700,001	to	$750,000	$3,625

$750,001	to	$800,000	$3,875
$800,001	to	$850,000	$4,125
$850,001	to	$900,000	$4,375
$900,001	to	$950,000	$4,625
$950,001	and above		$4,875

Post 110% recoupment, Designer's minimum guarantee, prorated on the basis of an eight (8) performance week, shall rise to $1,250/wk, against a fixed AWC based on gross weekly box office receipts as follows:

$0	to	$300,000	$1,250
$300,001	to	$350,000	$2,031
$350,001	to	$400,000	$2,344
$400,001	to	$450,000	$2,656
$450,001	to	$500,000	$2,969
$500,001	to	$550,000	$3,281
$550,001	to	$600,000	$3,594
$600,001	to	$650,000	$3,906
$650,001	to	$700,000	$4,219
$700,001	to	$750,000	$4,531
$750,001	to	$800,000	$4,844
$800,001	to	$850,000	$5,156
$850,001	to	$900,000	$5,469
$900,001	to	$950,000	$5,781
$950,001	and above		$6,094

"Full Performance Week," "Weekly Profits," "Gross Weekly Box Office Receipts," "Recoupment," and "Weekly Breakeven" shall be defined as per the Dramatists Guild Approved Production Contract for Plays, and in any event shall be on a favored nations basis with all royalty participants. "Net Profits" shall not be subject to any right of recall or accumulation for additional companies.

In the event any week of paid public performances consists of fewer or greater than eight performances, the amounts of gross weekly box office receipts and the amount of designer's royalty shall be prorated accordingly.

Designer's royalty shall not be subject to any waiver, reduction, or deferral without the Designer's prior approval.

Producer agrees to pay Pension and Welfare, in addition to the above royalty, on all royalty payments directly to United Scenic Artists.

Should Producer wish to institute paying all royalty holders on the basis of weekly net operating profits (NOP), Designer shall receive a minimum weekly guarantee of $500 against 1% of weekly NOP.

NOTE: *More and more, agents for a "star" designer (extensive Broadway credits, multiple industry awards, especially Tony Awards) try to negotiate for their clients a royalty that is a fraction of a percentage point, say one half of one percent, or 0.5%, of GWBOR. I always try to resist this for a play, especially when there is only a single set involved. The solution? Prerecoupment, I gave the designer a minimum guarantee of $1,000 that covered him up to a gross of $300,000, my estimated breakeven (but which still "saved" me $500 at that point compared to half a percent of that gross, which would have equaled $1,500). This was just the guarantee; the full compensation was actually determined by a series of gross tiers above $300,000 in $50,000 increments, in each of which the designer was paid a sum equivalent to .5 percent of GWBOR of the midpoint value of that tier. (For example, if the gross was between $301,000 and $350,000, the designer would receive .5 percent of $325,000, or $1,625, meaning an additional $625 over his or her guarantee of $1,000). Postrecoupment, the designer got a bump both on the guarantee (now $1,250) and on the fractional percentage point (now .625 percent of GWBOR) used to determine the fixed amount for each tier.*

In determining any fixed weekly compensation such as an AWC, it is important to state in the contract that the amount stipulated is based on an eight-performance week. Thus it can be prorated in any week with fewer than (or more than, as sometimes happens during the Christmas holidays) eight performances.

3. **PAYMENTS.** All fee and royalty payments shall be made payable and sent to _____ Agency a/a/f _____ Design Ltd f/s/o _____, at _____, New York, NY 100___, Attn: _____. The Federal ID number for this Payee is _____.

For foreign productions of the Play hereunder under Producer's control, lease, or license, all fees, advances, and AWCs due the Designer shall be paid in US dollars, without deduction for currency exchange, bank charges, or transfer fees, in accordance with the attached banking instructions.

Designer hereby appoints _____ Agency, _____, New York, NY 100__, Attention: _____, as his sole and exclusive agent ("Agent") with respect to the Play and authorizes and directs Producer to make all payments due or to become due to him hereunder (and under any subsequent agreements with Artist regarding the Play) to and in the name of Agent and to accept receipt by Agent as full evidence and satisfaction of such payments. In consideration of the services rendered and to be rendered by Agent, Designer hereby agrees that Agent is entitled to receive and retain as its commission ten percent (10%) of all such proceeds. The appointment of _____ as Agent is coupled with an interest and shall be irrevocable. All per diem payments due to Designer and expense reimbursements may be made payable directly to Designer.

NOTE: *Boilerplate. Notice that per diem payments and expense reimbursements are not commissionable and should be paid directly to the designer.*

4. **SCHEDULE.** Producer and Designer agree that the fee provided in the attached United Scenic Artists contract shall cover all work by Designer through the Official Opening in New York City. Designer acknowledges that the Play is currently scheduled to commence rehearsals on or about _____, begin preview performances in New York City on or about _____, and open in New York City on or about _____. Designer agrees to be present at times mutually agreed upon by Producer and Designer.

NOTE: *For the avoidance of any doubt, it is always wise to clearly state the show's anticipated schedule. Most designers juggle multiple projects and really need to be clear on the key moments of a given show so as to avoid conflicts. See paragraph 12 on page 131 for language that attempts to deal with an unanticipated change in schedule.*

5. **ASSISTANT.** Producer agrees to engage a union assistant of Designer's choice (subject to Producer's approval) for a period of not more than five

weeks at the current USA minimum scale for an assistant. Should the production schedule change, Producer and Designer agree to reevaluate Designer's assistant requirements based on such change.

NOTE: *Every year, it feels like the number of assistant weeks a designer claims he or she needs on a project increases. I sometimes wonder (cynically) if this is because designers are taking on too many projects for the same time period and need to pay a lot of assistants to cover their partial unavailability while they collect multiple fees. And the more assistant weeks that can be passed on to the producer, the less the designer will have to pay someone out of his own pocket. In any case, a designer typically needs an assistant for research, drafting of the plans, covering the full load-in period at the theater, keeping track of the departmental expenses and generating the reimbursement paperwork, etc. I try to get the agent to agree to the least number of weeks possible. Bottom line? If it turns out it is not enough and the designer needs more help to get the job done, the money will be found. But it never hurts to make the designer feel he only has a strictly limited amount of assistant time!*

6. **RIGHT OF FIRST REFUSAL.** Designer will be offered the opportunity to be the Scenic Designer or to license his Scenic Design for any future first-class theatrical production produced, co-produced, leased, and/or licensed by Producer under terms and conditions to be negotiated in good faith (but in no event shall the fee be less than the stated fee indicated for Designer hereunder for other first-class productions).

Such right of first refusal applies individually to all future first-class theatrical productions in territories for which the Producer and/or his licensees or assignees holds the rights and is subject to the Designer's availability at the time of each respective offer to Designer in circumstances where a license is not desired by Producer.

NOTE: *Boilerplate. Any designer hired to design a Broadway show is going to demand the right to design, or license his original designs for, additional productions under the producer's control.*

7. **REIMBURSEMENT OF EXPENSES.** Producer agrees to reimburse Designer for blueprints, fax, photocopying, transportation, and similar

reasonable related production expenses upon presentation of organized, itemized receipts.

NOTE: Boilerplate.

8. **BILLING.** Producer agrees to afford Designer billing credit in first position, on a line together with only other Designers on the title page of all theatre programs, house boards, advertising, and/or publicity matters under the Producer's control wherever and whenever the name of the other Designers appear. Such credit shall be of the same size, type, quality, format, and boldness accorded to the Costume Designer, Lighting Designer, and Sound Designer but not less than 25% of the average height of the title of the Play and shall be in the following form:

Scenic Design By

_____

Wherever credits are accorded in connection with the Play in a so-called "billing box" pursuant to which Designer is entitled to credit, the size of Designer's credit shall be determined by the size of the title of the Play in said billing box. Producer shall be entitled to accord so-called "movie credit" (i.e., run-on) billing in lieu of a billing box, provided all persons other than stars billed above the title and the director are so billed in such movie credits.

Producer further agrees that if the Costume Designer, Lighting Designer, and/or Sound Designer of the Production is listed and/or pictured in the biographical section of the so-called *Playbill* Program and/or the Souvenir Program for the Play, Designer will be afforded a listing and/or likeness of proportional prominence in the biographical section directly before the Costume Designer. The final draft of Designer's biography for use in all programs shall be submitted to the Designer for approval, which shall not be unreasonably withheld, and initialing.

No casual or inadvertent failure to comply with the foregoing requirements shall be deemed a breach hereof, unless same cannot and shall not be rectified prospectively and promptly after Producer's receipt of written notice from Designer specifying same.

NOTE: *In the theater, the accepted practice is for the set designer to receive first place billing among all the designers, the costume designer to receive second place, the lighting designer to receive third place, and the sound designer to receive fourth place.*

9. **HOUSE SEATS.** It is agreed that one (1) pair of House Seats, in good orchestra locations, will be held for purchase by Designer or his designee for each performance of the Play, except for theatre party, press performances, Tony voter, or benefit performances, commencing with the first paid public performance. Per Producer's contract with the theater, said House Seats will be used or released 96 hours prior to the scheduled performance. All House Seats shall be purchased at the regular box office price and shall be held for Designer's use by the General Manager's office. Designer's House Seat allocation and purchase procedure shall be on a favored nations basis with all other designers of Play.

NOTE: *Up until a few years ago, house seats were always released on a forty-eight-hour basis. But if a show was not a smash hit and selling out every performance, the danger was the choicest orchestra seats were being released back for sale to the general public on too-short notice. This often resulted in their not being sold at full price and winding up being sent to the same day TKTS booth, where they were heavily discounted. The solution was to release unused house seats ninety-six hours prior to a given performance and increase their chance for being purchased at full price.*

10. **OPENING NIGHT.** It is further understood that at least two (2) pair of orchestra seats will be made available for purchase by the Designer and one (1) complimentary pair (including party passes) for the New York City Opening Night. Designer's opening night ticket allocation shall be on a favored nations basis with all other designers of Play.

NOTE: *Any assistant who worked on the show will also be offered a pair of complimentary seats.*

11. All drawings, designs, and other specifications in digital and tangible media are the sole property of the Designer. Producer shall not have the right to assign, lease, sell, or license the rights to record, directly

or indirectly, the Scenic designs and/or scenery on film, tape, or by any mechanical means, in whole or in part, without the prior written approval of Designer. The fee for such approved use will be subject to negotiation with Designer. In addition, Designer shall have the option of supervising the execution of his original design and/or the redesigning of his original design for a film or tape-recorded version of Producer's production of the stage play (but not with respect to a theatrical or television motion picture based on the Play) at a rate to be negotiated in good faith.

It is understood, however, that Producer shall have the right to authorize the use of the scenic designs and the scenery created hereunder for the sole purposes of exploiting and publicizing the production of the Play in ways approved under Actors' Equity Association's Media Promotion and Publicity and Other Recording and Broadcast Provisions, including, but not limited to, in connection with excerpts of the Play, not exceeding fifteen minutes, to be broadcast on television for the purpose of publicizing the then current stage productions of the Play, or for award presentations, provided Producer and other personnel hired by Producer (excepting performers and other union personnel) received no compensation therefore other than reimbursement for out-of-pocket expenses, or on the Play's official website.

NOTE: Boilerplate.

12. In the event of any delay or postponement of a preview or opening date during the New York engagement due to scheduling changes and/ or changes in Artists, Staff, and/or Concepts which create conflicts in Designer's schedule that would not have occurred otherwise, Designer agrees to use his best efforts to fulfill his obligations to production, dependent on such schedule conflicts, and if necessary to designate an appropriate Assistant or Associate so that work can continue in Designer's absence.

NOTE: Much different from an actor or director, the majority, but certainly not all, of a designer's contribution is completed well before rehearsals begin, once the design has been approved, a scenic shop has been selected, and it is clear no design modifications are required. It is therefore possible, should a delay or postponement arise that results in the designer's unavailability, that a trusted surrogate will be able to step in for them and complete the process, checking in on the build at the scenic shop or handling any notes from the director once the scenery has been installed in the theater.

13. **TRAVEL AND PER DIEM.** In the event Designer shall be required by Producer to be more than 100 miles from his residence in New York City in connection with his services hereunder, Producer shall furnish to Designer round-trip economy air transportation (for scheduled flights of 3 hours or less in duration; business class air transportation for scheduled flights of more than 3 hours in duration); and hotel plus one hundred ($100.00) dollars per diem. Designer shall receive business class air transportation in the event of a production in the British Isles and hotel plus one hundred (£100.00) pounds per diem. In the event Designer' services are required in Los Angeles (or any other such location where the use of an automobile is mutually agreed to be reasonably necessary for local transport), Producer shall reimburse Designer for the use of a mid-size rental car, including minimum insurance, and basic work-related expenses—i.e., fuel, parking, and tolls.

All of Designer's terms and conditions regarding travel, housing, and per diem shall be on a favored nation's basis with all other designers of Play.

NOTE: Economy class is traditionally acceptable for flights of three hours or less. It is important to modify this with the word "scheduled," to preempt a claim that due to a delay in the flight beyond the producer's control, the party must now be offered more expensive airfare!

14. It is agreed that Designer shall not be responsible for damages resulting from failure of third parties to execute the Scenic Design, nor shall Designer be responsible in any way for delays due to strikes, accidents, acts of God, fire, or causes beyond the control of Designer. Designer agrees to supply all appropriate and necessary information to all third parties.

NOTE: Boilerplate.

15. Producer hereby agrees to cause Designer to be named as an additional insured on all liability insurance policies carried by Producer, and Producer agrees to deliver to Designer an irrevocable policy or certificate therefore.

NOTE: This paragraph provides for one of the additional insured certificates referred to in a previous chapter.

16. Notwithstanding the above, Producer agrees to release, indemnify, and/or hold harmless Designer with respect to any claim or demand for loss, damage, and/or injury to property, person, or thing rented, owned, or brought into theatre by Producer.

NOTE: Boilerplate.

17. If any or all rights convened herein above are assigned, Producer agrees to make such assignment only if his successor agrees to comply with, protect, and hold sacred the items and conditions by which the original Producer acquired the rights from Designer.

NOTE: I have always loved the standard language here, which promises that any successor to the Producer will "hold sacred" those items and conditions agreed to by the Producer! It bestows a grandeur on the proceedings that seems suitable to a religious rite.

18. **WARRANTY AND INDEMNIFICATION.** Designer warrants and represents that the designs will not infringe upon the rights of any third party; that Designer has the right to enter into this agreement and is not subject to any obligation or disability which will prevent or interfere with the performance of all the covenants to be performed by Designer under the Agreement; that Designer has not made, nor will make, any grant or assignment which will conflict with or impair the complete enjoyment of the rights and privileges granted by Designer under the Agreement; and that designs of the Designer are wholly original with Designer or in the public domain. Designer agrees to indemnify, defend, save, and hold Producer, Producer's heirs, executors, successors, administrators, and assigns harmless from and against any and all liabilities, damages, costs, expenses, and/or other losses (including reasonable attorney's fees) whatsoever which Producer may suffer by reason of any breach of the representations and warranties set forth in this paragraph.

Producer agrees to defend, indemnify, and/or hold harmless Designer from any third-party claims against Designer with respect to Producers production and exploitation of the Play except claims related to Designer's breach of Designer's representations and warranties set forth herein.

NOTE: Once again, note how these warrants and indemnifications are reciprocal, each party offering them to the other.

19. Any controversy or claim arising out of or relating to this Agreement, or the breach thereof, shall be settled by expeditious arbitration in New York City in accordance with the rules of the American Arbitration Association, and the United Scenic Artists shall be a party to such arbitration. Such arbitration shall be settled by a single arbitrator and judgment upon the award rendered by said arbitrator may be entered in the highest court of the forum, State or Federal, having jurisdiction thereof. The arbitrator is authorized to assess the defaulting party for the reasonable counsel fees and expenses incurred by the nondefaulting party in connection with the arbitration proceeding.

NOTE: Boilerplate.

20. In the event of a breach of this agreement by Producer, Designer's remedies shall be limited to money damages; in no event shall Designer have right to seek or obtain injunctive relief, and any arbitrator appointed under this agreement shall be bound by this provision.

NOTE: Boilerplate. The show must go on, so any action to remedy a breach is limited here to money damages, precluding any attempt to stop performances.

21. No party to this agreement shall be deemed to have breached any provision hereof, unless and until the other party hereto has sent written notice to said party specifying said party's failure in respect of any provision, and said failure is not corrected or rectified within five (5) business days after party's receipt of such written notice from the other party.

NOTE: Boilerplate. This paragraph provides for a cure to the breach and also requires that the designer initially inform the producer of a breach in writing.

22. This agreement shall be personal and nonassignable as to Designer (except that he shall have the right to assign his rights and obligations hereunder to a corporation of which he shall be the sole shareholder provided that he shall personally render the services required hereunder).

NOTE: Boilerplate. Again, this language links the services of the individual to his or her loan-out corporation.

23. No waiver by either party of, nor any failure by the other party to keep or perform, any covenant or condition of this agreement shall be deemed a waiver of any such preceding or succeeding breach nor of any covenant or condition of this agreement.

NOTE: Boilerplate. Each breach is individual in its scope and remedy and does not impact any other part of the agreement.

24. This Agreement shall be governed by the Agreement made between United Scenic Artists Local 829 and the Broadway League (or its successor agreements), the terms and conditions of which shall apply with respect to all additional first-class companies hereunder. Except to the extent the terms and conditions of this Rider and/or any other applicable collectively bargained agreement are more favorable to the Designer than the terms and conditions of the USA-League Agreement, in the event of a conflict, the USA-League Agreement shall control.

NOTE: Boilerplate. This paragraph incorporates all of the terms and conditions of the USA agreement governing it.

25. Designer or Designer's designee shall have the right to audit Producer's books and records on reasonable notice during regular business hours. Should any such audit reveal an underpayment greater than ten percent (10%) made by Producer to the Designer on any sums contractually due to Designer, the Producer shall bear the full expense of the audit.

NOTE: Boilerplate.

26. In the event Producer utilizes Designer's designs in the manufacture and sale of commercial merchandise to be sold in connection with Producer's production of the Play—i.e. T-shirts, hats, key chains, housewares, novelties, coffee table books including pictures, etc., Producer and Designer shall negotiate appropriate compensation therefore in good faith, commensurate with current royalties paid to designers of similar plays.

NOTE: *Boilerplate.*

27. Designer's services shall be rendered on a nonexclusive basis during the term hereof and subject always to Designer's prior professional commitments. The Designer's actual schedule shall be mutually determined by the Designer, the Director of the Play, and the Producer.

NOTE: *The designer is covering his, er, tuchus.*

28. Should Producer request Designer to perform additional services in connection with the production at a Broadway theater after the official opening of the play, Producer agrees to pay the Designer the prevailing minimum daily rate as determined by United Scenic Artists, prorated for four-hour work calls, for each day his/her services are rendered in connection with the production. For purposes of this Agreement, additional services shall not include so-called routine check-ins or teleconferences regarding maintenance of the design.

NOTE: *The designer is receiving an ongoing fixed royalty, or AWC, so the producer should not have to pay additionally for routine check-ins or teleconferences.*

All notices to any party hereunder shall be in writing and shall be deemed given when personally delivered or when mailed by first-class mail or express courier (such as Federal Express) in the continental United States (postage prepaid) or when transmitted and confirmed by telecopier. Copies of all notices to Designer shall be sent to: _____ Agency, _____, New York, NY 100__, Attn: _____.

Copies of all notices to Producer shall be sent to: _____
Broadway LLC, c/o _____, _____, New
York, NY 100__, Attn: _____.

This Agreement supersedes all prior agreements, oral or written, between
the parties with respect to the subject matter hereof; constitutes the entire
understanding of the parties; shall be construed in accordance with the
laws of the State of New York; may be modified only by a writing signed
by all of the parties; and shall be binding upon and inure to the benefit of
the respective heirs, executors, administrators, successors, and assigns of
the parties.

AGREED TO AND ACCEPTED: AGREED TO AND ACCEPTED:

_____ DESIGN LTD.   _____ BROADWAY LLC
F/S/O _____

_____   _____
_____, Designer   _____, General Manager

RIDER TO UNITED SCENIC ARTISTS' STANDARD SET DESIGN CONTRACT FOR _____ DESIGN LTD F/S/O _____ (CONTRACTOR) BETWEEN _____ BROADWAY LLC (PRODUCER) AND _____ (DESIGNER) FOR "_____" (PLAY). THIS RIDER DATED_____.

Whenever and wherever the provisions of this Rider differ from or conflict with the printed portion of this contract, the provisions of this Rider shall prevail.

1. It is understood and agreed that all references to Designer in the contract and Rider dated _____ shall be applicable to Contractor.

2. Contractor acknowledges that it is executing this contract as an independent contractor and shall perform and discharge all obligations imposed under all Federal, State, or local laws, orders and regulations in connection with the services of the Designer furnished by Contractor to the Producer. Contractor further agrees that the Designer shall be and remain during the Term hereof a member of United Scenic Artists and will perform services hereunder in accordance with the terms and conditions of United Scenic Artists Standard Set Design Contract for Broadway Productions. Contractor and Producer agree that the rules and regulations of United Scenic Artists shall be applicable as they may apply to this Contract, and agree respectively to comply with such rules and regulations and the terms of the attached United Scenic Artists Standard Set Design Contract for Broadway Productions and Rider as they apply.

The Producer agrees to make Pension and Welfare payments on the gross weekly payments for the services of Designer in accordance with United Scenic Artists Rules as they may apply and to make additional payments which may be due or become due the Designer pursuant to United Scenic Artists regulations as they may apply to this Contract.

_____ DESIGN LTD   _____ BROADWAY LLC
F/S/O _____

8

Sample General Manager Letter of Agreement

NOTE: Unlike company managers, who belong to ATPAM, general managers do not belong to a union. Because there is no union contract face to attach a rider to, their employment contract is in the form of a **letter of agreement (LOA)**.

Broadway Show LLC
c/o GM's Office
___West _Street, 5th Floor
New York, NY 10019

Date here

Name of GM
Corporate Name
Street Address
City, State Zip

RE: Insert Name of Play

Dear _____:

This letter will serve as our agreement setting forth your engagement by _____ (the "Producer") on a nonexclusive basis as General Manager, as such term is commonly understood in the theatre industry, for the forthcoming Broadway production now referred to as _____ (the "Play"), currently contemplating production in _____.

1. We hereby hire you, and you agree to be so hired, as the General Manager of the production company that presents the Play. You shall perform your services with due diligence and to the best of your ability. Although we acknowledge that you may act as general manager for other theatrical productions during the term hereof (whether or not of a competing nature with the Play), you agree to devote such time and attention as may be required fully to discharge all of your duties and obligations hereunder.

NOTE: *Many GMs manage multiple shows simultaneously, so if a given production is not their sole client, that show's producer needs to be reassured that the GM will devote enough attention to his or her project to do a fully competent job. I once had two shows happening more or less simultaneously, with barely two weeks separating their respective key dates—first rehearsal, load-in, first preview, and opening night. To make matters worse, both shows happened to star someone named Alan (Alan Bates in* Fortune's Fool *on Broadway and Alan King in* Mr. Goldwyn *Off Broadway), and both had the identical support teams working on them— the same lead producers, attorney, press agent, advertising agency, payroll service, insurance broker, casting agent, etc. In order to maintain my sanity and keep my focus, I found myself starting each conversation with "Please identify the show we are talking about!"*

2. You shall upon signing of this Agreement prepare itemized production and weekly budgets for this production based upon specifications for production related by us to you, or revise those budgets currently in hand, based upon a contemplated change of venue for the Play.

NOTE: Invariably, the first thing a producer wants a GM to tell them is "How much is it going to cost?" i.e., "How much money will I have to raise?"

3. You shall have the obligation and responsibility, to the extent specifically directed by the Producer, to negotiate, administer, and supervise all contractual and financial procedures on behalf of the production company, including banking transactions with signature on the so-called "general manager's account." You shall, if requested by the Producer and subject to the Producer's prior approval in each instance, contract and hire all required theatre and production personnel when they become necessary. All fees and royalties contracted for shall be and shall remain within the production and operating budgets, or as specifically approved by us should they exceed the original budgeted amount. You shall, as and to the extent requested by the Producer, negotiate, or assist in the negotiation of, all contracts for artistic personnel, performing or otherwise. As between you and us, the choice of such artistic personnel shall rest solely with us. You shall be responsible for paying all company bills out of the company accounts; shall cause all necessary tax returns to be filed properly on time; shall assist in the negotiating for rental of a theatre; shall supervise the sale of all tickets and box office procedures; and shall, in conjunction with the production company's accounting firm, render a weekly profit and loss statement of the company's operation, including an itemized accounting for all production expenditures. You shall make yourself available to the Producer for consultation at all reasonable times prior to and during the run of the Play.

NOTE: A GM is given a tremendous amount of responsibility and is repeatedly asked for his or her counsel and advice. Ultimately, however, all financial liability lies with the producer, and he is under no obligation to take a GM's advice. This can be very frustrating! In the end, if a GM feels a producer is not listening to his advice and is behaving in an irresponsible (usually as relates to fiscal matters) fashion, the only recourse a GM has is to quit the show. There are a lot of one-shot producers out there, but a GM is in for the long haul and depends on his or her relationships and good name to survive in the industry.

4. (a) For your providing your services to the production as General Manager, and for those facilities enumerated herein, you shall receive for your entire aggregate compensation for the initial company the following:

(i) pre-production fee of thirty-two thousand five hundred ($32,500) dollars, payable as follows:

(A) eight thousand ($8,000) dollars upon signing.

(B) eight thousand ($8,000) upon being asked to negotiate the theater contract or six months from the date of signing this contract, whichever occurs sooner.

(C) the balance of sixteen thousand five hundred ($16,500) dollars payable not later than two (2) weeks prior to the date of first rehearsal.

Notwithstanding the above, Producer is not obligated to produce the Play, nor is it obligated to produce it in the _____. In the event that the production is postponed or rescheduled beyond the aforementioned _____, then the schedule of payments above will be changed appropriately in direct relationship to the pushback. If Producer abandons Play, then all obligations hereunder will cease as of the date of any such abandonment, except for any fee/salary or expenses not yet paid to General Manager but already vested as per the payment schedule above.

(ii) a weekly salary of three thousand two hundred fifty ($3,250) dollars per week commencing at least two weeks prior to the week of first rehearsal and continuing until at least two (2) weeks following the closing of the run, but in no event later in starting or sooner in ending than the Producer receives his weekly producer fee.

(iii) should you need, included as part of the weekly compensation listed in 4 (a) (ii) above, to put yourself on an ATPAM contract as a second Company Manager, Producer agrees to pay for all appropriate minimum union benefits thereon.

(iv) should the Attorney General determine that an audit of the show is required after the run of the show has ended, you shall receive an additional three thousand two hundred fifty ($3,250) dollar fee for each audit required.

(b) The compensation set forth above will not include payment for the services of a Company Manager accountable to you whom you will choose with our prior approval. Company Manager's salary will be at

ATPAM minimum scale, unless we specifically consent to any higher salary. Company Manager's services and compensation will commence and terminate when required by ATPAM rules, unless Producer agrees otherwise. Producer hereby preapproves _____ as Company Manager.

(c) If, in connection with your duties respecting this or any other productions of this Play, we require you to leave New York City, you shall receive full reimbursement for all actual and reasonable transportation (ground and air travel economy class), hotels, meals, and ground transportation within each city. Should Author or Director have the right to travel by other than economy class, you also shall have the right to travel and be reimbursed for the same such travel class.

(d) You agree to make the facilities of your office, at _____ Street, _____ Floor, New York, available to each production of the Play on a nonexclusive basis during the entire preproduction, production, and performance period of the Play for which you shall receive a fixed weekly office charge as reimbursement for office operational expenses (which shall not include long-distance calls, pro rata share of local telephone calls, messengers, photocopying, fax charges, postage, express mailings, or any other legitimate, itemized show-specific expenses, for which Producer shall be separately billed), at the rate of one thousand two hundred fifty ($1,250) dollars per week, such payment to commence at the same time as the Producer's office charge commences, but no later than two weeks prior to the week of the first rehearsal, and to terminate no sooner than two (2) weeks after the closing or abandonment of each production of the Play, or until the Producer office charge is paid, if longer than two (2) weeks.

NOTE: As mentioned previously, a GM's production fee is usually paid in installments, the scheduling of which is negotiable. This fee is all the compensation the GM will receive until his or her weekly fee begins, generally two weeks prior to the start of rehearsal, even though this preproduction period could last a year or even several years. The weekly fee is separate from a weekly office fee, which is intended to help defray the GM's operating expenses—office rent, staff, utilities, telephone, service contracts for computers and copier machines, etc. If it is determined an audit is required, a tremendous amount of additional work can be generated for a GM, which is why a separate fee is negotiated for that eventuality. Finally, because GMs do not belong to a union, in order for them to receive health insurance, pension, and annuity contributions, it is common practice for them to go on a second company manager contract through ATPAM. (Most, but not all, GMs rise through the ranks by first becoming an ATPAM company manager and benefiting from a GM's guidance and tutelage).

5. The term of this Agreement shall be for the run of the Play of each production of the Play for which you serve as General Manager. The above notwithstanding, the Producer may, by written notice, terminate the General Manager for just cause, without compensation to the General Manager, except for any fee/salary or expenses then accrued. "Just cause" means, with respect to General Manager or _____, the breach of any material term of this Agreement and failure to correct such breach within 10 business days after written notice by the Producer to the General Manager of commission thereof. General Manager shall have the right to terminate this Agreement by providing Producer with four (4) weeks written notice, in which event General Manager shall receive no further compensation after termination of this Agreement.

NOTE: *Any good contract should contain language providing for how it can be terminated!*

6. We acknowledge that your creative contributions in the administrative aspects of mounting this production will be of great benefit to the anticipated success of this theatrical project. You shall receive billing as General Manager, equal in size to that accorded to the designers, in the announcement ad for the production, on all posters, window cards, 3-sheets, or 1-sheets in which the designers are accorded credit, on the title page of the program, and in the first position in the credit section of all theatre programs, souvenir books, and other staff listings relating to this production and all other productions on which you serve as General Manager.

NOTE: *Even a general manager has to think about his billing! These are standard terms.*

7. If this production or other companies of the Play shall open as a first-class production in another city within the United States or Canada, or be produced as a first-class national tour, or open in another country as a first-class production or tour, all under the control of the Producer, then you shall have the right of first refusal to serve all such productions as General Manager under all of the terms and conditions, financial and otherwise, of this Agreement. Your original preproduction fee of thirty two thousand five hundred ($32,500) dollars, weekly salary, and office charge shall be equal to that in effect for the original production. In all other respects, all other considerations shall be no less favorable to you than the terms in effect under this Agreement. If other second-class companies of the Play open, such as a bus-and-truck or college tour, and are under the control of the Producer, you shall have right of first refusal to serve all such productions as General Manager under terms and conditions to be negotiated in good faith. The foregoing terms shall not apply to productions under license to another production company.

NOTE: Mounting a show for the first time is a lot of work. If a GM makes that happen, and the show is successful, the GM wants to be sure he or she has the right of first refusal to work on future productions.

8. If, in our sole discretion, your services shall be required following the close of the final production of the Play in order to make periodic distributions of funds to investors, maintain the continuing records of the production relating to subsidiary or other income, handle bank deposits and arrange for the issuance of financial statements, etc., you shall receive an annual payment of three thousand two hundred fifty ($3,250) dollars at the close of each fiscal year during which said services have been required. After two such fiscal years, Producer and General Manager agree to review this annual compensation in good faith and reevaluate this payment based on such standards as income coming in to Play, distributions made to investors, etc. It is never the intention of the General Manager to receive the payment of an annual fee that would cause the producing entity to enter into a negative cash balance.

NOTE: If a show is successful, it is likely the original producing entity will participate in the author's subsidiary income streams for many years to come—as an example, stock and amateur distributions will be made twice a year, checks to the partnership will be sent c/o the general manager's office, statements will have to be reviewed and the entity's financial share double checked, bank deposits will have to be made, distributions will be calculated for investors, cover sheets will be written, mailings will be collated, stuffed, stamped, and mailed out, end of year accounting statements will have to be reviewed and sent to investors, as will individual tax reporting forms, etc. Once the show has closed and the GM has been paid his two week close-out fee, no compensation is paid to him or her for maintaining ongoing details, other than the annual fee stated above.

9. Nothing in this Agreement shall be deemed to create a partnership, joint venture, or similar relationship creating liability on your part. You are not responsible for any debts, costs, etc., of the production company unless incurred or expended by you outside the scope of your authority hereunder, and you are not to be considered a partner or joint venturer. We shall indemnify and hold you harmless from and against any and all charges, expenses, claims, liabilities, and risks that you may incur because of any demands or claims made against you by reason of the production and presentation of the Play by us. We shall have the right to defend any such claim with counsel of our choosing.

NOTE: Boilerplate.

10. Any controversy or claim arising out of or relating to this Agreement, or the breach thereof, shall be settled by expeditious arbitration in New York City in accordance with the rules of the American Arbitration Association. Such arbitration shall be settled by a single arbitrator, and judgment upon the award rendered by said arbitrator may be entered in the highest court of the forum, State or Federal, having jurisdiction thereof. The Arbitrator is authorized to assess the defaulting party for the reasonable counsel fees and expenses incurred by the nondefaulting party in connection with the arbitration proceeding.

NOTE: Boilerplate.

11. In the event of a breach of this agreement by Producer, your remedies shall be limited to money damages; in no event shall you have the right to seek or obtain injunctive relief, and any arbitrator under this agreement shall be bound by this provision.

NOTE: Boilerplate.

12. No party to this agreement shall be deemed to have breached any provision hereof, unless and until the other party has sent written notice to said party specifying said party's failure in respect of any provision and said failure is not corrected or rectified within five (5) business days after party's receipt of such written notice from the other party, except (a) to an entity in which Producer and/or any of its principals is a general partner, managing member, joint venturer, controlling stockholder, or principal, provided such entity assumes in writing the Producer's obligations hereunder; or (b) to you or to an entity controlled by you, provided such entity assumes in writing your obligations hereunder and you remain bound to provide the services set forth herein on behalf of such entity.

NOTE: Notice the breach provision also provides for its cure—any breach can be corrected or rectified within five business days of receipt of the written notice informing of the breach.

13. If any or all rights convened herein above are assigned to an entity, such as an LP or LLC, which has been formed to produce Play and in which Producer serves a leadership role, such as a General Partner or Managing Member, Producer agrees to make such assignment only if the successor entity agrees to comply with, protect, and hold sacred all the items and conditions which the original Producer has agreed to herein. Additionally, you shall have the right to assign your right to receive any portion of payments due to you hereunder.

NOTE: Boilerplate.

If the foregoing constitutes your full and complete understanding of the terms and conditions of your employment, please sign below where indicated and this letter shall act as our agreement.

ACCEPTED AND AGREED TO: ACCEPTED AND AGREED TO:
A Broadway Show LLC.   _____

_____   _____
By: _____, Managing Member   _____, President
                                 Fed ID # _____

9

The Producing Entity—What It Owns, Choosing Its Form, Setting It Up, and How It Works

Producing a Broadway show involves legally establishing a new financial entity. This entity makes an offering to potential investors and provides the mechanism for them to invest in the production. This offering is often referred to as a syndication. Establishing this entity is an involved process that is really a series of collaborations between the production attorney and the GM, with each party taking the lead responsibility for different steps along the way.

But even before the producing entity can be established, the producer has to obtain the right to produce the play from the author.

This is accomplished through a document called an **option agreement**, traditionally drafted by the production attorney. This document grants the producer the exclusive right to produce an identified dramatic property (the Play) in a specific area (Territory) within a limited period of time (Term) for a particular sum of money (Option Payment). There will be prenegotiated term extensions requiring additional option payments if the process takes longer than anticipated.

On Broadway, should the producer succeed, within his or her term, in raising the money and opening the play with a minimum of ten consecutive previews plus an official press opening, then the producer is deemed to have **vested** in the property (i.e., earned the right to additional opportunities). Vesting qualifies the producer to elect a series of subsequent production rights if he or she so chooses, as well as to participate in a share of the author's subsidiary income from sources of exploitation that were originally reserved by the author. The Dramatist Guild's **Approved Production Contract** (**APC**) for plays also offers definitions of vesting that require differing amounts of performances to qualify but give credit for out-of-town performances and performances in the British Isles, Australia, and New Zealand.

Subsequent production rights are prenegotiated rights that allow the producer to produce, lease, or license the play in the original territory (the United States, Puerto Rico, and Canada) outside of New York City, in additional territories (the British Isles, Australia, and New Zealand), and in any supplemental territories (for example, Germany, France, China, or Japan) that were agreed to in the option agreement. Each of these territories will require its own option payment to secure the exclusive production rights, and the producer will have a set period of time after initially vesting in which to announce his intention to exercise these rights.

Because it is recognized that a successful Broadway production has contributed significantly to the overall value of other rights in the property, vesting, as described in the preceding paragraph, also allows the original production entity to share in the author's **subsidiary income**— income the author receives from sources such as media productions (a film sale, or a made-for-television movie), stock and amateur licensing, ancillary productions (such things as a concert tour version of the show, a musical adapted from the show, Equity productions classified as "theater for young audiences" or "small professional theaters", etc.), commercial use products (apparel, novelties, souvenir books, etc.), and revivals. The APC offers the producer four different alternatives for subsidiary income participation to choose from, each one outlining a different formulation of what percentage of each source of revenue the production entity will share in for a specified period of time (for example, 50 percent of media productions in perpetuity, 50 percent of stock performances for the first five years, then 25 percent for the next three years, but 0 percent of amateur and ancillary performances). One choice favors stock over amateur participation, while another does just the opposite, and the producer must elect in writing which formula he or she is choosing no later than the end of the first day of rehearsal. It is important, therefore, that the producer have a clear sense of where the property will have the most value in its life after Broadway.

Since the option agreement has to be secured before the entity can be formed, the option is usually taken out by the lead producer personally, and the rights obtained are subsequently assigned to the entity in which the producer is a managing member or general partner.

Once the rights have been obtained, the producing entity can be formed. The entity is normally organized either as a limited liability company (**LLC**) or a limited partnership (**LP**). There are pros and cons to each form of entity, with particular repercussions in the areas of liability protection for the producer(s) and the operating costs of the entity.

In the area of liability, the producer, in an LP, assumes the role of a general partner, while the investors are limited partners. An investor's liability is limited to the amount of his investment and he has no exposure beyond that, while an individual general partner has unlimited liability for any and all debts of the partnership. One way for the producer to protect himself from this exposure is to form a business entity with limited assets to serve as the general partner of the LP. In this instance, the producer's personal assets are not vulnerable to the claims of any potential creditors.

In a limited liability company, in contrast, liability is treated similarly to the way it is in a corporation—creditors only have access to the entity's assets, not those of any individual members. So the producer, referred to in this instance as a managing member, has no personal exposure whatsoever.

Regarding relative costs, LPs formerly had a financial advantage over LLCs in that they had lower initial filing fees that were required for their formation. Over the years, changes in tax laws have reduced these costs for LLCs, thereby equalizing the formation costs for the two entities.

As for comparative maintenance costs, especially in the area of annual filing fees, again, this used to represent a significant difference between these two forms, but over time the laws have changed, diminishing the discrepancy. New York State tax laws require an annual filing fee for

LLCs, but not for LPs. For LLCs, the cost was formerly calculated on a per member basis, at a fixed rate of $50 a member, but more recently the calculation has been changed so that it is now based on the show's New York source income (essentially, net adjusted gross box office receipts and any merchandise sales), with annual fees ranging from a minimum of $25 (for income up to $100,000), to a maximum of $4,500 (for annual income in excess of $25,000,000!). This change greatly benefits LLCs, whose shows have ceased operating on Broadway but remain open as an entity in order to receive subsidiary income from the author. Under the new guidelines, the cost of their annual filing fee will adjust, and be lowered, as their new source income is similarly reduced, resulting in a fee that could be as low as $25 annually.

One last variable to weigh when deciding whether to form an LP or LLC is whether or not one expects the show to ever play in Canada, perhaps as a pre-Broadway stop or as an extension of a national touring company. Canada does not recognize an LLC and treats it as a corporation, which means an individual who had been a managing member suddenly has exposure to any of the entity's liabilities.

Once its form has been agreed upon, the production attorney files certified Articles of Organization for the producing entity with the NYS Department of State, in their Division of Corporations and State Records, and obtains a Filing Receipt in exchange. The entity now officially exists.

Here is where the GM gets involved. The next crucial step is to obtain an employer identification number (EIN), sometimes referred to as a federal ID number, for the newly formed entity. This can be done via phone or Internet, utilizing the Internal Revenue Service's website, where the necessary Form SS-4 is readily available.

Not until the entity has an EIN can a bank account or accounts be opened, and checks, deposit slips, and endorsement stamps ordered. This falls within the GM's purview. A Broadway show usually has a minimum of two bank accounts—a general checking account and an interest-bearing money market account for any temporary surplus—and sometimes a third, separate payroll account as well. The address for the producing entity will be in care of the GM's office, since that is where all bills and bank statements are sent.

At this point, the entity has been formed and bank accounts are open. But before the producer can begin accepting money from investors, the production attorney has to draft official investment documents—an operating agreement and subscription documents (the latter of which consists of a Subscription Agreement and a Purchaser Questionnaire, which determine if an investor meets certain suitability standards to become an investor in the company). In New York State, the production attorney then has to file Form 99 with the state's attorney general within two weeks of the first financial offer, and Form D with the Securities and Exchange Commission. Additionally, the attorney is required to file a form, the equivalent of New York State's Form 99, in most other states in which securities are offered depending on the requirements of the particular state.

When investment papers are sent out to investors, it is usually requested that they be returned with checks (if funds are not wired directly into the show account) in care of the GM's office. This is so the GM can review the paperwork, which is complicated and has many different components, all of which have to be correctly filled out and signed, and deposit and record the amount of investment. A producer often asks the GM for an update on how the capitalization is coming along, and when completed, the GM will have executed a worksheet that shows what percentage of the whole each individual investor's contribution represents. This worksheet can then be extended, so that in the event of a profit distribution, it will calculate what part of the total sum being distributed each investor will receive, be it a return of capital or a distribution of net profits. Finally, using this same worksheet, the GM can use the names and addresses of the investors to create mailing labels and mail merges.

While the investors' capital is being returned, up until the point where production costs have been recouped, investors will receive their pro rata share of 100 percent of the money being distributed. Once production costs have been recouped, however, the show is in net profit, and the investors receive 50 percent of the profits, the other 50 percent going to the producers. If, however, the producer has contractually agreed to pay certain key artistic personnel (i.e., the director, a star, a nonprofit theater that aided in the development of the property by giving it a full-scale production) a percentage of net profits, these profit points traditionally come off the top, resulting, after their deduction, in an adjusted net profit figure, which is then split 50/50 between investors and producers. By way of example, if the producer has collectively granted creatives a total of 5 percent of net profits, which come off the top, then the net profits that started at 100 percent are now reduced to adjusted net profits of 95 percent, and the investors and producers each share in half, or 47.5 percent, of this amount.

NOTE: Recoupment is accomplished by accumulating enough profit to equal the show's production expenses, not its full capitalization. That means that at the point of recoupment, investors will not have received 100 percent of their money back, as the production expenses are only part of, and therefore less than, the total capitalization. Most shows make a big deal about achieving recoupment, sending out press releases to announce this proud accomplishment. But I once worked for a producer who worried that her investors would not understand why the show had recouped and was now into net profit, when they had not yet received all of their investment back. She therefore instructed us not to breathe a word of our having recouped to anyone! A producer's wish is a GM's command, but I found this situation so frustrating that I secretly created a screensaver for my computer monitor that bemoaned, in moving text, "The unspeakable shame of recoupment!"

Although the producers retain 50 percent of adjusted net profits, it is important to note that they may assign points from their personal share of these net profits to anyone they wish. As the costs of producing a show have risen, and it has become increasingly difficult to raise larger and larger amounts of capitalization, it has become common practice for the lead producers of a show to offer an additional incentive to large-scale investors, or to those who assist them in raising a significant portion of the financing. This incentive takes the form of extra net profit points from the producer's own share of profits. This incentive is traditionally calculated as a fraction of the investment points the sum of money invested or raised represents, with the return improving as this sum increases. For example, if the investment represents 5 percent to less than 10 percent of the capitalization, the producer may offer a return of 1 percent of his or her net profits for each 4 percent of capital raised. This is called a "1 for 4" deal. If the money represents 10 percent to less than 25 percent of capitalization, it may qualify for a "1 for 3" deal. Finally, if the investment is 25 percent or more of the capitalization, it could be rewarded with a "1 for 2" deal. In this last instance, if an investor put in 50 percent of the total capitalization, he or she would get an additional 25 percent of adjusted net profits from the producer and wind up owning 75 percent of adjusted net profits.

10

Programming the Box Office

The best financial insurance a show can have is strong advance ticket sales. The best way to build an advance is to put the show on sale as soon as possible and to advertise its existence to the public. The best (and only!) way to put the show on sale is to give the theater owner all the information needed to program his or her computers, so tickets can be sold online, over the phones, and, usually at a later date, at the box office window. Studies have shown that the majority of sales are now conducted over the Internet and phone, and the activation of these two venues, collectively referred to as "going on soft sale," is far less expensive per week than opening the box office. Once the show goes on hard sale and the box office is opened, it triggers a variety of union salaries (not only the treasurers themselves but also a stage doorman and a porter) plus benefits and payroll taxes and additional theater expenses such as utility charges.

The information needed to program a show and put it on sale for the general public is extensive and comprehensive. Not only do you have to know what your performance schedule is and what your regular ticket prices are, you also have to specify which seat locations should *not* be put on public sale but must be reserved for company and theater house seats (prime location seats held for the exclusive use of various creative personnel, such as the stars, author, director, designers, and producer) for both regular and theater party performances (explained later in this chapter), for opening night seats, for critics performance seats, and for company seats during previews, when creative staff will need to watch the show and take notes from the back of the house. You also need to determine which locations will be sold as **premium seats**—choice location orchestra seats sold to the general public at a higher price than regular orchestra seats—and what changes to your playing schedule will occur around opening night and upcoming major holidays. Below is a sample set-up memo, followed by various worksheets and charts referred to in the memo, which will give an idea of the complexity and detail of the information that has to be conveyed.

....

NAME OF SHOW
c/o General Manager's Office
Street Address
City, State Zip
Telephone: ;   Fax:
Email:

TO: _____ (name) / _____ (email)
CC: _____ (name) / _____ (email)
FROM: _____ (GM name)
RE: _____(show name)/ Box Office Set-Up Information
DATE: _____, 20__
pp: _____

Show: SHOW NAME HERE
Theater: _____
Production Co: _____ Broadway LLC, c/o GM Office
Phone: ( ) _____ ext. ___, fax: ( ) _____
General Manager: _____ Company Manager: _____
    phone: ( ) _____ ext. ___, fax: ( ) _____

Press Agent: _____ Agency   Rep: _____
           phone: ( ) _____, fax: ( ) _____
Advertising Agency: _____ Agency Acct. Rep: ____
phone: ( ) _____, fax: ( )
Website: www._____.com
Written by: _____
Directed by: _____
Starring: _____

Description of show: Official, approved show description here. This will be used by all telephone sales agents and will appear on the show website as well. It is important that the production provide its own copy, so the show is described the way the producer wants it to be described.

Total Time Of Performance (two acts): approximately ____ hours, ____ minutes, including intermission.

Type of Show: Play
Audience: no one under the age of 7 admitted

NOTE: This first section serves as a brief "cheat sheet" for all sales personnel, either treasurers at the box office or operators at telephone sales centers such as Telecharge or Ticketmaster. It helps them answer many of the basic questions the public is likely to ask and gives them the name and contact information for key personnel if they need to contact a show representative on any matter.

Telecharge Open: Friday, June 26, 2015—phones and online only
Box Office Open: Friday, November 6, 2015—for all customers (2 weeks prior to 1st Preview)
Performance Schedule:
Tues at 7 p.m.
Wed at 2 p.m.and 7 p.m.
Thurs at 7 p.m.
Fri at 8 p.m.

Sat at 2 p.m. and 8 p.m.
Sun at 3 p.m.
Dark Mondays
Exceptions: CANCEL: Sunday, December 6 at 3 p.m.
                     ADD: Monday, December 7 at 7 p.m.
                     CANCEL: Sunday, December 13 at 3 p.m.

NOTE: The show normally has a Tuesday evening through Sunday matinee performance schedule, with Monday as the "dark day" or day off. Opening night is scheduled on a Thursday, to strategically push reviews into the Friday papers, which are heavily read as people look forward to the upcoming weekend. Traditionally, at least three dates are offered to critics to review the show prior to its opening night ("critics performances"), ideally at the beginning of the weekly playing schedule when the actors will be fresh and at their best. To accommodate all of this, for the week of opening night only, it was decided to have the show play on a Monday, when it is normally dark, and, in order not to give nine performances that week, to have a compensatory dark day the following Sunday, when there would normally be a performance. This, in turn, resulted in cancelling the regular Sunday performance prior to the added Monday one, so the cast would have a chance to recharge before running the final gauntlet of critics' performances and opening night.

Thanksgiving Holiday Schedule:

CANCEL: Thursday, November 26 at 7 p.m.
ADD: Friday, November 27 at 2 p.m.

Christmas Holiday Schedule:
CANCEL: Thursday, December 24 at 7 p.m.
CANCEL: Friday, December 25 at 3 p.m.
ADD: Sunday, December 27 at 7 p.m.
ADD: Monday, December 28 at 7 p.m.
ADD Tuesday, December 29 at 2 p.m.
CANCEL: Thursday, December 31 at 8 p.m.

NOTE: Thanksgiving Day is normally a soft performance, as the majority of people gather at a friend's or family member's home and don't go out. The next day, Friday, is a holiday for many people, and an added matinee performance that day will usually be well attended. That said, an uplifting, entertaining show is more likely to sell out than a dark, edgy one. The period immediately prior to Christmas is also traditionally weak for sales, with people's time taken up dashing to holiday parties and frantically buying last-minute gifts. Conversely, the period between Christmas and New Year's is usually the most lucrative week of the entire year, now that people are in full holiday swing and eager to have a good time. For this reason, the labor unions have allowed shows to alter their regular playing schedules at Christmas so that they can perform seven shows in the week prior, followed by nine shows the next. The above specified holiday schedules, with their added and cancelled performances, address both these holidays' concerns.

1st Preview:
Friday, November 20 at 8 p.m.

1st Night Press Performances:

Monday, December 7 at 7 p.m.	75 Pairs
Tuesday, December 8 at 7 p.m.	75 Pairs
Wednesday, December 9 at 7 p.m.	75 Pairs

2nd Night Press Performances:

Tuesday, December 15 at 7 p.m.	75 pairs
Wednesday, December 16 at 7 p.m.	75 pairs
Thursday, December 17 at 7 p.m.	75 pairs

See separate sheets for specific holds for these dates.

Opening Night:
Thursday, December 10, 2015 at 6:30 p.m. Please keep all of the Orchestra *off sale* except for the following locations, which you *should* put on sale *at the premium price of $225*:

Orch row F: 9 – 15 and 10 – 16
Orch row G: 9 – 15 and 10 – 16

Orch row J: 15 – 17 and 16 – 18
Orch row K: 15 – 17 and 16 – 18
Orch row L: 15 – 17 and 16 – 18
plus all four boxes.

In addition, please take the **Front Mezzanine (A – C) off sale** for this performance at this time.

NOTE: Cast, crew, producers, the author, the director, the designers, investors, the theater owner, celebrities, and press all have to be accommodated with good seats on opening night. For this reason, the best seats in the house are kept off sale from the general public and reserved for the use of the show and the theater owner, who contractually receives a set number of opening night tickets.

Tickets On Sale Thru:
Sunday, February 21, 2016 (ten full playing weeks after week of Opening Night). After every week of sale, please put one additional week on sale, so the show is always on sale only for ten weeks at a time.

NOTE: This is called a rolling sales period—as one week is played off at the beginning of a cycle (in this case ten weeks long), an additional week is added at the end. The hope is to keep ticket sales tight, so that the advance sales are concentrated over a relatively small number of weeks and not spread out over too long a period of time. I once managed a show that had revolving casts of stars that changed every four weeks. We had to put multiple casts on sale at the same time, but ticket buyers bought seats for a date based on which stars they wanted to see, even if that performance were many months away. While our overall advance figure looked very robust, a breakdown of the advance showed that this large amount of money was actually spread very thinly over too many weeks, not significantly helping each individual week to get close to its breakeven point.

Regular Ticket Prices:
All prices are prior to the inclusion of the $1.50 theater facility fee.
See attached Price Scale for Regular Pricing.

Seats Locations to Be Taken Off Sale:
TBD

NOTE: Some seats may need to be marked as unavailable for concerns such as the sound board, which is often placed in the back of the orchestra, necessitating the removal of seats, or for sightline problems, which sometimes affect extreme side seat locations that, once the set is installed and sightlines are reviewed, are deemed to have an obstructed view of the stage.

House Seats: See attached chart.

<u>Regular</u> (40)   <u>Party</u> (26)

All Regular and Party locations are 96-hour release unless indicated that they are 6 p.m., same day status.

NOTE: Party locations are a reduced pool of regular house seat locations, which come into play on dates when the group sales for larger theater parties require more choice locations than are readily available and regular house seat locations are needed to help fill the order. The majority of house seats are held until ninety-six hours (till 6 p.m. of the fourth day) prior to a given performance and, if unused at that time, are then released for sale to the general public. To accommodate same-day VIP requests, a small number of house seats are held on a 6 p.m. release basis (12 noon for matinees). If the show is a huge success, sold out and with a waiting list for returns, chances are the theater will hold a few emergency pairs as well, releasing them five or ten minutes before curtain. The box office treasurers are granted discretion in using their best judgment to maximize ticket sales, striving always to achieve the highest possible gross and have as few seats as possible go dead (unsold).

Premium Seat Locations:
30 for all perfs—see attached chart.

Production Seats: 20 (for Preview Perfs 11/20–12/09)

O 101–104   111–114
N 101–104
M 2–4 M 1–3
L 2–4   L 1–3

If the house is selling out, consult with company manager about releasing some of these locations and selling them.

Groups Sales:
Early Bird Special: order (and pay in full) by the first performance, Nov. 20, 2015—40% discount off all Regular Prices, good for all performances 11/20–2/21/16, except for the following black-out dates: 11/26–11/29/15, 12/24/15–1/03/16. Subject to availability.

NOTE: There are blackout dates for group discounts during the choice Thanksgiving and Christmas/New Year's holidays. Also, discount offers of any kind always should contain the disclaimer "Subject to Availability," so that if the demand for full-price tickets increases, the show can instruct the box office to shut off the discount at any time. This information is usually printed in very small size type, which within the industry is referred to as "mice type"!

10% commission, except for Saturday nights

WE WILL LET 8 PEOPLE CONSTITUTE A GROUP.

Price Keys:
All prices are *before* the inclusion of a $1.50 facilities fee.
See attached Price Scale for all Regular and Premium Prices.
$63.50 Direct Mail

Please let me know the ticket code you assign to the Direct Mail piece ASAP, as it needs to go into the copy of the mailer. The parameters are as follows:

Direct Mail: $63.50 price (plus $1.50 facility fee on top). Offer drops October 16. Must order by December 10 for performances through December 23. Good at BO and via Telecharge. Limit of eight tickets per performance. Good for all performances, subject to availability.

We will be submitting Price Key and code requests for additional discount offers as the need arises.

Press Seats

If any of our press seat locations go unused and are released, please use your discretion and convert them to additional premium seats as per the attached price scale if you feel there is a need for them.

Thank you.

NOTE: *The preceding set-up memo discusses the following worksheets and seating charts. These samples illustrate the various details one must consider when programming the box office.*

Sample Regular Show House Seat Pull

		96 Hour		6:00 PM
Author	4	**D 101 - 104**	2	D 110 - 111
Director	4	D 110 - 113	2	D 112 - 113
Star 1	4	E 111 - 114	2	**G 101 - 102**
Star 2	4	**G 101 - 104**	2	G 103 - 104
Actor	2	J 105 - 106		
Actor	2	J 107 - 108		
Press	6	F 111 - 114		
		D 2 - 4	2	F 2 - 4
Producer	4	F 2 - 4		
		G 2 - 4		
Producer	2	G 111 - 112	2	G 111 - 112
Producer	2	G 113 - 114	2	G 113 - 114
General Manager	6	J 2 - 4	2	G 2 - 4
		C 1 - 3		
		C 2 - 4		
Set Designer				
Costume Designer				
Lighting Designer				
Sound Designer				

REGULAR PERFORMANCE

		B
		D

REGULAR HOUSE SEAT CHART

Broadway Play House

Orchestra

REGULAR PERFORMANCE

A		
C		

										AA				111	110	109	108	107	106	105	104	103	102	101	AA									
			11	9	7	5	3	1		A				111	110	109	108	107	106	105	104	103	102	101	A	2	4	6	8	10	12	14		
		13	11	9	7	5	3	1		B			112	111	110	109	108	107	106	105	104	103	102	101	B	2	4	6	8	10	12	14		
		13	11	9	7	5	3	1		C		113	112	111	110	109	108	107	106	105	104	103	102	101	C	2	4	6	8	10	12	14		
		13	11	9	7	5	3	1		D		113	112	111	110	109	108	107	106	105	104	103	102	101	D	2	4	6	8	10	12	14		
		13	11	9	7	5	3	1		E	114	113	112	111	110	109	108	107	106	105	104	103	102	101	E	2	4	6	8	10	12	14	16	
	15	13	11	9	7	5	3	1		F	114	113	112	111	110	109	108	107	106	105	104	103	102	101	F	2	4	6	8	10	12	14	16	
	15	13	11	9	7	5	3	1		G	114	113	112	111	110	109	108	107	106	105	104	103	102	101	G	2	4	6	8	10	12	14	16	
		13	11	9	7	5	3	1		H	114	113	112	111	110	109	108	107	106	105	104	103	102	101	H	2	4	6	8	10	12	14		
17	15	13	11	9	7	5	3	1		J	114	113	112	111	110	109	108	107	106	105	104	103	102	101	J	2	4	6	8	10	12	14	16	18
17	15	13	11	9	7	5	3	1		K	114	113	112	111	110	109	108	107	106	105	104	103	102	101	K	2	4	6	8	10	12	14	16	18
17	15	13	11	9	7	5	3	1		L	114	113	112	111	110	109	108	107	106	105	104	103	102	101	L	2	4	6	8	10	12	14	16	18
17	15	13	11	9	7	5	3	1		M	114	113	112	111	110	109	108	107	106	105	104	103	102	101	M	2	4	6	8	10	12	14	16	18
17	15	13	11	9	7	5	3	1		N	114	113	112	111	110	109	108	107	106	105	104	103	102	101	N	2	4	6	8	10	12	14	16	18
	15	13	11	9	7	5	3	1		O	114	113	112	111	110	109	108	107	106	105	104	103	102	101	O	2	4	6	8	10	12	14	16	

Mezzanine

Left | Right

25	23	21	19	17	15	13	11	9	7	5	3	1	A	114	113	112	111	110	109	108	107	106	105	104	103	102	101	A	2	4	6	8	10	12	14	16	18	20	22	24	26
25	23	21	19	17	15	13	11	9	7	5	3	1	B	114	113	112	111	110	109	108	107	106	105	104	103	102	101	B	2	4	6	8	10	12	14	16	18	20	22	24	26
25	23	21	19	17	15	13	11	9	7	5	3	1	C	114	113	112	111	110	109	108	107	106	105	104	103	102	101	C	2	4	6	8	10	12	14	16	18	20	22	24	26
25	23	21	19	17	15	13	11	9	7	5	3	1	D	114	113	112	111	110	109	108	107	106	105	104	103	102	101	D	2	4	6	8	10	12	14	16	18	20	22	24	26
25	23	21	19	17	15	13	11	9	7	5	3	1	E	114	113	112	111	110	109	108	107	106	105	104	103	102	101	E	2	4	6	8	10	12	14	16	18	20	22	24	26
25	23	21	19	17	15	13	11	9	7	5	3	1	F	114	113	112	111	110	109	108	107	106	105	104	103	102	101	F	2	4	6	8	10	12	14	16	18	20	22	24	26
25	23	21	19	17	15	13	11	9	7	5	3	1	G	114	113	112	111	110	109	108	107	106	105	104	103	102	101	G	2	4	6	8	10	12	14	16	18	20	22	24	26
25	23	21	19	17	15	13	11	9	7	5	3	1	H	114	113	112	111	110	109	108	107	106	105	104	103	102	101	H	2	4	6	8	10	12	14	16	18	20	22	24	26
25	23	21	19	17	15	13	11	9	7	5	3	1	J	114	113	112	111	110	109	108	107	106	105	104	103	102	101	J	2	4	6	8	10	12	14	16	18	20	22	24	26
25	23	21	19	17	15	13	11	9	7	5	3	1	K	114	113	112	111	110	109	108	107	106	105	104	103	102	101	K	2	4	6	8	10	12	14	16	18	20	22	24	26

Balcony

A	23	21	19	17	15	13	11	9	7	5	3	1
A	23	21	19	17	15	13	11	9	7	5	3	1
B	23	21	19	17	15	13	11	9	7	5	3	1
C	23	21	19	17	15	13	11	9	7	5	3	1
D	23	21	19	17	15	13	11	9	7	5	3	1
E	23	21	19	17	15	13	11	9	7	5	3	1
F	23	21	19	17	15	13	11	9	7	5	3	1
G									7	5	3	1

A	112	111	110	109	108	107	106	105	104	103	102	101
A	112	111	110	109	108	107	106	105	104	103	102	101
B	112	111	110	109	108	107	106	105	104	103	102	101
C	112	111	110	109	108	107	106	105	104	103	102	101
D	112	111	110	109	108	107	106	105	104	103	102	101
E	112	111	110	109	108	107	106	105	104	103	102	101

A	2	4	6	8	10	12	14	16	18	20	22	24
A	2	4	6	8	10	12	14	16	18	20	22	24
B	2	4	6	8	10	12	14	16	18	20	22	24
C	2	4	6	8	10	12	14	16	18	20	22	24
D	2	4	6	8	10	12	14	16	18	20	22	24
E	2	4	6	8	10	12	14	16	18	20	22	24
F	2	4	6	8	10	12	14	16	18	20	22	24
G	2	4	6	8								

Legend:

Company House Seat Holds (includes 6 Press)
Theater House Holds (48) (20 during Previews)
Theater Contractual (Playbill/ Runyon/ Actor's Fund)
Premium Seats (30)

101 Aisle Seat with Folding Armrest
101 Wheelchair Viewing
101 Companion
Low Vision

PARTY PERFORMANCE

PARTY PERFORMANCE CHART

Broadway Play House

Orchestra

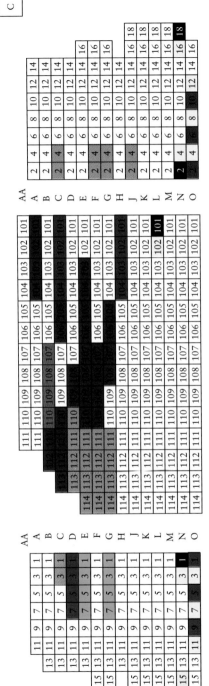

Mezzanine

Right

Left

PARTY PERFORMANCE

Balcony

23	21	19	17	15	13	11	9	7	5	3	1	A
23	21	19	17	15	13	11	9	7	5	3	1	B
23	21	19	17	15	13	11	9	7	5	3	1	C
23	21	19	17	15	13	11	9	7	5	3	1	D
23	21	19	17	15	13	11	9	7	5	3	1	E
23	21	19	17	15	13	11	9	7	5	3	1	F
								7	5	3	1	G

112	111	110	109	108	107	106	105	104	103	102	101
112	111	110	109	108	107	106	105	104	103	102	101
112	111	110	109	108	107	106	105	104	103	102	101
112	111	110	109	108	107	106	105	104	103	102	101
112	111	110	109	108	107	106	105	104	103	102	101

A	2	4	6	8	10	12	14	16	18	20	22	24
B	2	4	6	8	10	12	14	16	18	20	22	24
C	2	4	6	8	10	12	14	16	18	20	22	24
D	2	4	6	8	10	12	14	16	18	20	22	24
E	2	4	6	8	10	12	14	16	18	20	22	24
F	2	4	6	8	10	12	14	16	18	20	22	24
G	2	4	6	8								

101 Aisle Seat with Folding Armrest
101 Wheelchair Viewing
101 Companion
Low Vision

Company House Seat Holds (26, includes 4 Press)
Theater House Holds (12)
Theater Contractual (8-Playbill/ Actor's Fund)
Premium Seats (30)

Sample Party Performance Reduced Show House Seat Pull

		96 Hour		6:00 PM
Author	2	D 110 - 111		
Director	2	D 112 - 113	2	D 112 -113
Star 1	2	E 111 - 112		
Star 2	2	E 113 - 114	2	E 113 - 114
Actor				
Actor				
Press	4	F 111 - 114	2	G 113 - 114
Producer	4	F 2 - 4		
		G 2 - 4		
Producer	2	G 111 - 112		
Producer	2	G 113 - 114	2	F 113 - 114
General Manager	6	C 1 - 3	2	C 1 - 3
		C 2 - 4		
		J 2 - 4		
Set Designer				
Costume Designer				
Lightning Designer				
Sound Designer				
	26		10	

PRESS PERFORMANCES
Pre & Post Opening Press (75 PAIR / 150 TICKETS)

Legend:
- 101 — Aisle Seat with Folding Armrest
- 101 — Wheelchair Viewing
- 101 — Companion
- Low Vision

For Dates:

Pre-Opening:
1 Monday, December 7 at 8 PM
2 Tuesday, December 8 at 8 PM
3 Wednesday, December 9 at 8 PM

Post-Opening:
4 Tuesday, December 15 at 7 PM
5 Wednesday, December 16 at 7 PM
6 Thursday, December 17 at 7 PM

Press Pull

A Broadway Theatre
1,050 seats

Scale 1:   Tues–Thurs eves @ 7 PM, Wed mat @ 2 PM

Orchestra	422	seats at	140.00	$59,080.00
Premium Orchestra	0	seats at	225.00	$0.00
Mezzanine A–E	200	seats at	140.00	28,000.00
Mezzanine F–K	200	seats at	95.00	19,000.00
Mezzanine Boxes	16	seats at	95.00	1,520.00
Balcony A–G	212	seats at	65.00	13,780.00

1050	$121,380.00
Less 0.045	5,462.10
Less League Dues	136.50
	$115,781.40
Number of Performances	4
	$463,125.60

Scale 2:   Fri @ 8, Sat @ 2 & 8 PM, Sun @ 3 PM

Orchestra	422	seats at	150.00	$63,300.00
Premium Orchestra	0	seats at	250.00	0.00
Mezzanine A–E	200	seats at	150.00	30,000.00
Mezzanine F–K	200	seats at	105.00	21,000.00
Mezzanine Boxes	16	seats at	105.00	1,680.00
Balcony A–G	212	seats at	75.00	15,900.00

1050	$131,880.00
Less 0.045	5,934.60
Less League Dues	136.50
	$125,808.90
Number of Performances	4
	$503,235.60
SUBTOTAL	$966,361.20
Less .05 Commission	48,318.06
TOTAL	**$918,043**
average ticket price:	$109.29

* **A $1.50 Facilities Fee will be added to the established price of each ticket**

11

Employees—Their Hiring, Set Up on Payroll, and Responsibilities

Once a GM has negotiated the terms for someone's employment, the individual has to be officially hired and set up on payroll. This requires sending the person (or his agent, as the case may be) mutually reviewed and approved contracts or letters of agreement (**LOA**), which the GM, as the employer's representative, has signed first. If the person has an agent, there will be at least three (employee/employer/agent) copies and, if he or she belongs to a union like Equity, possibly as many as five to be countersigned. If the individual has a loan-out company and belongs to a union, there may be as many as five places to sign on each of the five copies, twenty-five signatures in total! All the places where a signature is required should be clearly indicated. Additionally, when the contracts go out for signature, the appropriate hiring forms—a W-4 and I-9 for individuals who will be paid a salary, and a W-9 for a corporate entity being paid a fee—should be included, as well as explicit instructions that the forms be completed and returned along with the appropriate countersigned contracts. The completed hiring forms will contain the name of the person or entity being hired, the applicable social security number or federal ID, as well as an address, marital status, and the number of exemptions declared for tax withholding. These forms must also provide proof that an individual is not an illegal alien.

Calculating, submitting, checking, and distributing the payroll on a weekly basis is ultimately the job of the company manager, whose employment begins shortly before rehearsals commence. But in order for the company manager to submit a company payroll for the first week of rehearsals, the GM needs to have already set up the payroll account and obtained a payroll number.

There are a handful of excellent payroll companies that specialize in the theatrical industry—its unions, their dues, vacation and benefit rates, and their separate benefit funds (pension, health, annuity). It is wise to use such a company, rather than a generic payroll company with no particular knowledge of the commercial theater, and I strongly advise you to do so. Most GMs have a preference for a specific company they know and trust, and the GM typically selects the payroll company to be hired.

Once the company has been hired, they will have specific set-up procedures to be followed. This initially entails giving them the company name, EIN (see chapter 9), address (c/o the GM office), the contact information for various personnel, and the details of the appropriate, linked checking account—the account name, bank name and address, account number, and routing number—that the payroll checks will be drawn on. The payroll company will then create a payroll number to identify the particular show. A payroll company will have a variety of forms one can utilize—to set up a new hire, to reactivate a rehire, to record a prepay (an early fee installment, manually issued prior to payroll being run, but still needing to be recorded by the payroll service so it can be included in end-of-year tax reporting), to cancel a previous payment, to record a change of address, etc.

Most payroll services have their own employee handbook to guide you in setting up a payroll. Each person or entity being paid will have an account number that consists of three components: the show's payroll number, an individually assigned employee number, and a department number, with subcategories that indicate the union or classification involved and the particular subdivision within that area. For example, a numerical code may indicate the jurisdiction of Equity but only apply to stage managers, or it may indicate a section for royalties but be a subcategory that applies only to designers.

Particularly in a department that deals with unions, a theatrical payroll service is set up so that within that department, a union's given vacation rate is automatically calculated and added to the gross, and that union's specific due's rate is calculated and deducted from the gross. But to guarantee maximum flexibility, there are also options that can be elected that provide codes to override the default settings—one that stops vacation pay being added but still deducts union dues, one that stops vacation and union dues calculations, one that adds vacation pay but doesn't deduct dues, etc.

Before the company manager comes on board, therefore, the GM needs to have set up the payroll account, received a show payroll number, and kept track of all the prepays that will need to be reported. Once the GM has received the countersigned contracts and the completed hiring forms, the individual or entity can be paid promptly. If this is for someone who is contracted long before rehearsals begin—the author, or director, say—his or her check will most likely be "hand cut," that is, written directly from the check register and not issued by the payroll service. In that event, a prepay form recording the payment can be simultaneously prepared and held in a folder, to be sent in to the payroll company and processed by them once weekly payroll begins running.

In 2011, New York State passed the Wage Theft Protection Act, meant to protect vulnerable, possibly non-English-speaking workers from financial abuse by unscrupulous employers. The Act applies to all employees paid a salary (not to independent contractors or corporations paid a fee) across the board. The fulfillment of the Act's requirements necessitates a mountain of paperwork on the employer's behalf, which is traditionally added to the company manager's already heavy load. There are two primary components: an initial notice and acknowledgment of employment rates, and a weekly wage statement to accompany each employee's paycheck.

The initial notice and acknowledgment of employment terms is a form that must go to every individual who is paid a salary. It must be submitted to the employee upon hire or within ten business days of the first day of his or her work. The form must state the employee's regular rate of pay and the basis of that pay, be it hourly, by shift, by day, per week, salary, or something other. If the individual is eligible for overtime, his or her hourly and overtime rates of pay must be stated, as must be the pay day and whether the payment is for the current week or retroactive for the previous week. Additionally, this form must give the employer's name, address of principal place of business, mailing address, and telephone number. The employee must sign and date the acknowledgment and indicate he accurately identified his primary language. Ideally, this notice should be provided in English *and* the primary language identified by the employee, if different. The NYS Department of Labor has templates for this notice in English, Spanish, Chinese, Korean, Creole, Polish, and Russian! If the NYSDOL does not have a template for the primary language indicated, it is permitted to give it out only in English.

Once the employee has acknowledged all this information and signed the notice, the employer retains the original and gives the employee a copy. If the employee is covered by a collective bargaining agreement, as everyone is on Broadway, the notice must include rates applicable to the specific employee. The employer has to notify the employee of any reduction in his wage rate at least seven calendar days before it becomes effective. There are penalties to the employer for failure to provide timely notice. Retaliation by employers against employees is prohibited. And to top it all off, this notice and acknowledgment process has to be repeated annually!

On an ongoing basis, the employer is required to provide each employee with a wage statement on every paycheck stub he or she receives or on a separate document attached to each paycheck. This information must state how payments and deductions are calculated and give contact information for the employer: his name, address, and telephone number. The statement must include the employee's name, state the days worked that are covered by the payment, show the rates of pay and their basis (again, hourly, shift, day, week, salary, or other), give the gross and net wages, indicate any deductions made, give the regular hourly and overtime rates of pay for employees eligible for overtime, state the number of regular and overtime hours worked, and, upon request, provide a written explanation of how the payment was computed. This back-up is required for every employee, every week.

While certainly worthy in intent, the Wage Theft Protection Act is not really intended for union employees, who have many protections, checks, and balances already in place—printed union rulebooks that clearly state both the employee's and employer's responsibilities and lay out the negotiated minimum terms and conditions of employment, union representatives or deputies in the workplace whom one can easily turn to if one has concerns, standards of just cause that preclude frivolous or unwarranted job termination, union officials who will fight for their members and provide free legal representation if necessary, and a series of grievance and arbitration measures already in place to provide a forum for resolving labor disputes. There isn't a person working on Broadway who isn't represented by some form of union, guild, or society—except, ironically, the GM!

12

Binding Insurance

One of the many duties GMs do not directly do themselves but are none-theless responsible for overseeing is the securing of insurance for the show. This is done through an insurance broker, who obtains quotes on the policy premiums from various insurance companies. There are a handful of experienced brokers who specialize in theatrical insurance, and they are the ones who should be consulted.

While the range of specific insurance needs varies from show to show, there are six standard policies that pertain to just about every show and which are mandated by law, a union rule, a specific negotiated contract such as the theater lease, or plain common sense. In addition to these, a producer may elect to carry a number of other policies for a variety of different reasons. The most common of both of these kinds of policies are described below.

THE BASIC SIX

1. Theatrical Package
This is literally a package of policies, consisting of the following four basic components.

Theatrical Property

Specifically insures the replacement value of the physical production elements—the set, props, costumes, wigs, lighting and sound equipment, etc.—the show either owns or is liable for. The cost of the set, props, costumes, and wigs are all costs that will naturally come to a GM's attention and are therefore easy for him or her to keep track of. The GM must be sure to ask the equipment rental shops, especially those for lighting, sound, and video, for the replacement value of the equipment package that is finally agreed upon, so these figures can be added to the total value of the physical production. As the various rental values are often not known until quite late in the process, after insurance has already been bound (acquired), the GM initially estimates these values based on prior experience, and once the real value is known, accordingly adjusts the total amount that the insurance policy must cover. If the total figure is now higher than the original estimate, this will, of course, affect the value of the insurance premium.

Performance Disruption (Also Known as Business Interruption)

Covers the actual business income loss and/or extra expense incurred due to the necessary cancellation, interruption, or postponement of one or more performances caused by outside conditions. The policy also covers the inability to open a new production as scheduled. This insurance applies only when the actual or potential disruption is caused by a covered occurrence, such as fire or civil authority (public closings ordered by the government in response to weather emergencies, terrorist attacks, a health epidemic, etc.). Performance disruption can also include catastrophe accident coverage, which is generally needed for touring productions. Typically this coverage has a two-performance deductible before it kicks in.

Equity Property Coverage

This is an example of a type of insurance mandated by a union contract—Actors' Equity Association (AEA or Equity). It covers direct physical loss or damage to personal property of employees caused by or resulting from a peril not otherwise excluded and is also available to nonunion employees. The limit per employee varies by the type of Equity contract, but a Broadway contract, for example, has a limit of $16,000 per employee.

Third Party Property Damage
Covers damage to real property that is in your care, custody, or control. Usually has a limit of $1,000,000.

2. COMMERCIAL GENERAL LIABILITY
This is the primary coverage that protects the show from bodily injury and property damage claims. This form of insurance will be required in your theater license, which will also stipulate different limits along the lines of: $1,000,000 for each occurrence, a policy aggregate of $2,000,000, a premises damage limit varying between $100,000 and $1,000,000, and a medical payments limit of between $5,000 and $10,000. A blanket additional insured endorsement should be included on the policy, which will allow for additional insured certificates to be issued. These certificates provide insurance to key individuals and entities affiliated with the production, such as the author, director, theater owner, designers, producers and coproducers, general manager, as well as lighting, sound, and scenic shops.

3. COMMERCIAL AUTO (HIRED AND NONOWNED AUTO LIABILITY)
Provides liability coverage for bodily injury or property damage due to your negligence while using a vehicle that is rented or borrowed or caused by an employee using his own vehicle on behalf of the business. This insurance normally comes with a limit of $1,000,000 for each occurrence/$1,000,000 in the aggregate. An accompanying component, hired auto physical damage, further covers claims to vehicles you rent.

4. COMMERCIAL UMBRELLA (OR EXCESS LIABILITY)
Provides you with additional limits of liability protection above and beyond the primary protections offered by the commercial general liability, commercial auto, and employer's liability policies. This can be useful if the liability limit of any of these other policies has been exhausted by a loss, if the show suffers liability exposure for which there is no primary insurance, or when a primary policy contains an exclusion that is not similarly excluded under the umbrella policy. It is also an economical way to purchase additional liability limits, as the minimum premium for each additional $1,000,000 is typically $1,000! Commercial umbrella is

another insurance required by the theater lease, which will usually demand the show carry a minimum of $10,000,000 in umbrella limits.

5. WORKERS' COMPENSATION

This is an example of insurance that is required by state law. Workers' comp, as it is commonly referred to, provides insurance for employees who are injured in the course of employment. The coverage pays for hospital and doctors bills, or death benefits, according to the various state laws. In addition to covering medical expenses, workers' comp will cover a percentage of the employee's lost wages should the injury result in the employee's inability to work.

Employer's liability is part of workers' compensation. It provides a limit of liability, varying from $100,000 to $1,000,000, from claims brought by the injured employee's dependents against the employer.

The workers' comp premium is arrived at by classifying employees into categories and providing estimated payroll for each applicable category at the start of the policy. When the show closes, an audit will be performed and the premium will be recalculated based on the actual payroll that was run. Since the norm is to originally calculate the payrolls on an annual basis (unless you know your show is going to have an announced, limited run for a shorter period), it is likely, if the show runs less than a year, that you will receive a partial refund on your premium. Note that if you hire any independent contractors, they must provide a certificate of insurance proving they have their own coverage, or they will be charged under your coverage at the time of the audit.

6. DISABILITY (ORIGINALLY REFERRED TO AS "ACCIDENT INSURANCE")

This is another statutory policy required by state law. Disability insures an employee against loss of income in the event of nonoccupational injury or illness that prevents one from working and provides 50 percent of lost wages up to $170 per week. Instead of having an upfront premium payment, disability is billed on a quarterly basis and calculated at a different, modest monthly rate for males and females—recently $2.90/month for males, $6.35/month for females.

FREQUENTLY ELECTED ADDITIONAL POLICIES

1. ERRORS AND OMISSIONS (E&O, OR PRODUCERS' LIABILITY)

Covers legal liability and defense for the production company against lawsuits alleging unauthorized use of titles, ideas, characters, plots, plagiarism, libel, slander, defamation of character, and invasion of privacy. Coverage can be extended to include merchandising for an additional premium. Coverage typically excludes preexisting claims (of which the insured had knowledge), breach of contract, and an act committed by the insured with knowledge that it violates the rights of others.

Acceptance of coverage for the title is dependent upon a satisfactory title search report, which confirms whether or not the play's current title is clear to be used. This requires a separate application that should be submitted two to six weeks prior to the first performance.

2. DIRECTORS AND OFFICERS (D&O)

D&O is a form of liability insurance paid to the directors and officers of a company, or to the entity itself, to reimburse losses or to advance defense costs in the event a legal action is brought for alleged wrongful acts performed by the entity's directors or officers. The insurance often also covers any financial settlement the entity makes, up to the amount specified in the policy.

This coverage can be extended to include employment practices liability, which covers such workplace allegations as wrongful termination, discrimination, and sexual harassment.

3. STAR INSURANCE

Star insurance comes in two basic forms.

Nonappearance

Offers protection against the loss of box office income or additional expenses incurred when a star misses performances due to circumstances beyond his or her control. Typical perils covered include death, accident, or illness. There are many different ways of structuring such a policy, either by setting a limit of insurance based on a specific gross one wants insured or by just covering the show's expenses. In any event, this policy will require a completed application, a copy of the capitalization budget, a copy of the weekly operating budget, a recoupment schedule, and a completed medical exam performed by an approved physician before full coverage can be secured.

NOTE: If a star is out, management always tries to convince patrons to come back to another performance and not seek a refund, but if the patron is adamant, and the star is billed above the title, one cannot refuse to return the money. I once managed a Broadway show starring Academy Award–winner Richard Dreyfuss, who had a bad back. One day the dreaded call came—Richard's back had gone out, and he would not be able to perform that evening. Hoping to troubleshoot, I went over to the theater prior to curtain to get the lay of the land. We had a number of well-known actors who were billed above the title, including the wonderful René Auberjonois, a Tony Award-winner himself, who also happened to be Richard's understudy. Seeing a small cluster of patrons discussing the situation, and sensing they were trying to decide if they should stay or ask for their money back, I approached them and introduced myself. "You know," I said, "we are probably the only show on Broadway that, when our main star is out, offers a Tony Award–winning actor in his place, not just Hymie Pippick." "Really?" they asked, impressed. "Yes," I explained, "René Auberjonois won a Tony Award for *Coco* opposite Katharine Hepburn and will be going on tonight in the role of Sly." "But doesn't he normally play another role?" they asked. "If he goes on for Sly, who goes on for him?" I paused, thought it over, then admitted "Hymie Pippick." Unabashed, I encouraged them to stay and see the show and promised them I would be in the lobby when the show got out. If they were still dissatisfied then, I would be happy to invite them back as our guests to a later performance. Happily, they exited having had a wonderful time, and we kept their money!

Abandonment

Provides coverage for the cancellation of an entire production when a key individual is unable to continue in his employment due to reasons beyond his control. Typical insured perils are again death, accident, or illness. The limit of coverage is usually tied to the show's capitalization costs. It is recommended that coverage be put in place once the production company begins spending money. The coverage term of the policy matches the term that the insured person is contracted to be with the production.

Such insurance might be considered if the show has an elderly player (director or star, most likely) who is vital to the project and deemed irreplaceable. Although this policy does not have a deductible, it has a two-week waiting period before a claim can be made, in order for the insurer to feel confident that the claimant really will be unable to return.

4. STORAGE (FOR THE PHYSICAL PRODUCTION ELEMENTS)

If, at the end of the show's run, there is hope of licensing the physical production to another theater, or talk of mounting a tour, then it is worthwhile to transport and store the physical production elements for possible future use. But if you are going to the trouble and expense of storing these items, you had better make sure you insure them!

Additional polices will be required for a show that tours in the US or Canada or travels to other foreign countries.

Although a GM does not secure insurance himself, he must understand the process, make sure he can have a dialogue with the broker about the show's needs, and see to it that insurance is put in place in a timely fashion. And whenever a contract with the show contains an insurance clause—for example, the license agreement with the theater, the rental agreement with the lighting shop, or a star actor or director contract—the GM has to make sure that section of the contract is relayed to the insurance agent.

13

Financial Overview

I like to joke that in show business, I'm the business half. More than any other function, the GM's primary responsibility is the management and forecasting of the show's finances. During the production period, this involves first budgeting the show, then recording the investment (capitalization) as it comes in, and finally keeping track of the estimated production expenses as they become finalized: How successful have the contract negotiations been? Which items have come in under budget? Which are over budget? How does that affect the bottom line? More specifically, what is the net effect of these variances on the budgeted reserve, which needs to be in place not only by the first preview but also as of opening night?

During production, one of the most effective methods of keeping track of millions of dollars of expenses is by converting the production budget into a cash flow chart. An example of such a spreadsheet is attached at the end of this chapter. To read it accurately, start with the column second from the far left, the original "Budget" column. From here, columns are added to the right—first for the total "Spent to Date," which gets updated weekly, then individually for each week between that date and the first preview, then for expenses "Still Expected" (remember, many production expenses may have a final installment date that is triggered by opening night, but even though they are technically paid out during the operating period, they are still accounted for as production expenses). The sum of these then appear in a "Total" column, and to its right is the final column, labeled "Over/(Under)," which compares this total to the original budget and shows at a glance which line items are on target, over budget (a positive number), or under budget (a negative number, in parentheses). If items are collectively over budget, the only place money can come from to pay for them is out of the reserve, thereby diminishing it. Conversely, collective savings go toward increasing the amount of the reserve. In the spreadsheet, note for example that the set (scenery) expense is $65,000 over budget, but the line item for broker fees is $24,000 under budget. Although some departments are over budget and others are under, the bottom line, shown in the lower right-hand corner, is that the entire show is coming in $49,264 *under* budget. At least at this point in time!

The chart is also invaluable for tracking the show's expected cashflow needs on a weekly basis. This can be accomplished by totaling the amount of anticipated expenses in each weekly column, as shown in the line second from the bottom. For example, in the column labeled "Week Ending 10/25/15," the estimated anticipated cash needed for that week is $429,619.

The show accountant should set up accounting codes for production and operating expenses that match up with the budget's line items, and these codes should be applied to every check that is written, so that it will be crystal clear how an expense relates to the budget and whether it is a production expense or a weekly operating expense. Sometimes a bill payment will require a split transaction, meaning the total amount due needs to be split between several expense codes (e.g., a bill from a lighting shop that contains charges for both perishables and trucking).

During the production period, the cashflow should be updated at the end of each week, after all that week's bills have been coded and issued. Once paid, the expenses in a given week should be transferred to the Spent to Date column to their left. Anything that was expected to be paid that week but wasn't should be moved forward (i.e., to the right) into a future week. Once a column has been cleared out, it can be eliminated, and the date of the Spent to Date column should be updated. Although the accountant will be doing a weekly update on production costs once rehearsals begin, he or she will only know about expenses that have been paid. The cashflow adds to these figures the still anticipated costs that are known to the GM, thus yielding a more accurate assessment of where the total costs are headed and how they relate to the budget.

At some point several weeks prior to the first preview, the GM needs to begin reviewing the breakdown of advance sales on a week-by-week basis. Computerized box offices can yield detailed reports for a myriad of data, including a report that tells you, on a performance-by-performance basis, the dollar value of advance ticket sales sold for that performance, the number of seats sold for that performance, how many unsold seats remain for that performance, and what the total **gross gross** (the box office revenue figure before contractually allowed deductions for things like credit card or group sales commissions reduce it to a **net gross**, on which royalties are actually paid) is for that week. By analyzing this, one can see quickly if it looks like the show will break even that week and which performances are likely to need help boosting their attendance—either through additional paid advertising, marketing promotions, increased publicity, sending tickets to the same-day **TKTS** discount ticket booth, offering discounted seats in advance to **Theatre Development Fund** (TDF) or, last resort, by discreetly comping (offering complimentary seats, or "**paper**") to targeted audiences. Although no one wants to give away free tickets, most shows need a minimum number of audience members for a performance to be effective. Audience members need to feel part of a large enough crowd to be comfortable enough to react freely and in turn fuel the actors' performances. In addition, a larger audience has the potential to generate more positive word of mouth, hopefully resulting in better paid sales down the road. Giving away comps is a gamble one hopes will turn into an investment.

A helpful tool for trying to predict future weekly grosses is a ten-week-out gross projection chart. An example of such a chart is included at the end of this chapter. Before one can begin forecasting for future weeks, one needs the data from a certain number of weeks that have already played out. The concept is to look at a given point in time for a future week—say, two weeks out—scan vertically up that same column until you find a prior, already played out week that had a similar gross at that same point in time, and see what gross that comparative week ended up with. Of course, you have to be mindful of special circumstances that could distort the comparison—you don't want to compare a holiday week with a nonholiday week, for example. To further illustrate, look on the chart at w/e (week ending) 2/22/15. At two weeks out, the week has an advance of $115,050. Scanning upwards, w/e 2/01/15 had a fairly comparable advance at that same point in time of $119,412 and wound up grossing $266,314. This is probably a better basis for projecting how w/e 2/22 will do than by comparing it to w/e 1/18/15, which, although it had a gross of $110,312 two weeks out, contained the weekend leading up to Martin Luther King Day. If you look at the growth in a week's gross over its final playing week, shown in the column to the right of the one showing the final net gross, you begin to get a sense of how much the gross typically grows over that period. W/e 1/18, containing a holiday weekend, grew just over $119,000 over the course of the week, which is considerably higher than the average growth for a regular, nonholiday week. Forecasts are never ironclad (if there unexpectedly is a blizzard and public transportation is closed, the projected growth rate of that week's gross is going to be severely slowed), but at least one can make intelligent guesses.

Another statistic that is looked at constantly and minutely dissected is the daily **wrap** figure. A wrap is the total amount of ticket sales sold on a given day, starting at one minute after midnight and ending at midnight the same day, from all sales sources (box office window, telephones, Internet, remote outlets). A wrap is broken down into all the possible types and prices of tickets that comprise it—full price, premium seats, group sales, coded discounts, direct mail, a specific email blast, TKTS, TDF, etc. Since the wrap represents the total amount of ticket sales for that day, if the show is already in performance, some of those sales will undoubtedly be same-day sales for that day's performance(s), while the balance will consist of advance sales for future dates. When the box office statement for each performance is finalized, the gross gross for that show is deducted from the total advance, since that part of the advance has now been played off. Conversely, at midnight, the day's final wrap is added to the advance. Thus, for a show's advance to keep growing, on any given day the amount of the total wrap added to the advance figure must be greater than the amount of any gross gross performance(s) deducted from it.

Since the wrap breaks out each type of ticket sold, and the discounts have been given identifying codes, the daily wrap can also be used to track the **return on investment** (**ROI**) of discount offers such as direct mail and individual email blasts—comparing the cost of the endeavor to the revenue it yielded. A sample tracking chart for advertising cost effectiveness is included at the end of this chapter. As an example, note that the first line shows a *Playbill* email blast that cost $15,000, which was coded and tracked and yielded $108,389.40 in revenue, a profit of $93,389.40.

While ad agencies should keep track of the effectiveness of the advertising and marketing they propose, it is important, on principle, that the GM keep his own records for analyzing these endeavors. Even expert advice needs to be checked and, if appropriate, challenged at times.

Budgets, cashflows, weekly advance breakdowns, gross projections, daily wraps, discount tracking—these are just some of the myriad financial reports that producers look to the general manager to provide them with. The worse a show's grosses are, the more anxious a producer understandably gets. After all, the producer is the one with the financial liability. This directly translates into the producer constantly requiring more and more financial reporting and forecasting. Providing all this information and analysis is a big part of the GM's job. If a GM's first duty is telling a producer how much a show will cost, one of his last duties is recommending that the show should close. This is not a pleasant task, but more than anyone else, the GM must be grounded in reality when the reserve is gone and losses are looming. I like to joke that the main arc of a general manager's job can be summed up by the words "This is what it's going to cost; now it's time to close."

SAMPLE BROADWAY CASHFLOW
(Preliminary & Tenative—for Discussion Purposes Only)

A Broadway Theater
1102 Seats

CAP: based on: 2,900,000 15th draft 08/01/16

	Budget	Spent to Date as of 10/11/15	1st reh 10/25/15	11/01/15	Load-in 11/08/15	11/15/15	1st Preview 11/22/15	11/29/15	12/06/15	ON 12/13/15	Still Expected	Total	Over/(Under)
PHYSICAL PRODUCTION													
Scenery	$250,000	150,000	50,000		85,000		30,000					315,000	65,000
Props/Dressing Rooms	65,000	15,975	20,000		8,025							44,000	(21,000)
Rehearsal Props	5,000		4,000									4,000	(1,000)
Rehearsal scenery	0	4,000										4,000	4,000
Costumes	35,000		10,000	10,000	7,000							27,000	(8,000)
Make-up/Hair	2,500		2,500									2,500	0
Special Effects	0											0	0
Electrics	6,000			6,000								6,000	0
Carp/Elecs/Sound (Perishables)	12,500	95			3,000	3,000	3,000	3,000	500			12,595	95
Sound (Prep/3 weeks rental)	4,000			4,000								4,000	0
Sound (Recording)	7,500		10,000									10,000	2,500
	$387,500	170,070	96,500	20,000	103,025	3,000	33,000	3,000	500	0	0	429,095	41,595

FEES	Budget	Spent to Date as of 10/11/15	1st reh 10/25/15	11/01/15	Load-in 11/08/15	11/15/15	1st Preview 11/22/15	11/29/15	12/06/15	ON 12/13/15	Still Expected	Total	Over/(Under)
Author (Option Payment)	0											0	0
Director	75,000	50,000			25,000							75,000	0
Executive Producer	35,000	25,000	10,000									35,000	0
General Manager	32,500	32,500										32,500	0
Scenic Designer	20,000	10,000					5,000			5,000		20,000	0
Costume Designer	6,380		3,190				1,595			1,595		6,380	0
Lighting Designer	9,815	2,450	2,450				2,450			2,450		9,800	(15)
Sound Designer	5,000		2,500				1,250			1,250		5,000	0
Tech Supervisor	18,000	4,500			4,500		4,500			4,500		18,000	0
Special Effects Designer	0											0	0
Press Pre-Production	7,500	7,500										7,500	0
Consulting Producer	25,000	10,000	5,000	5,000			5,000					25,000	0
Media Consultant	8,500	8,300										8,300	(200)
Casting Director	18,000	12,000	6,000									18,000	0
Fight Director	750											0	(750)
Dialect Coach	0		1,000									1,000	1,000
Hair Designer	0		1,000									1,000	1,000
Composer	7,500		5,000							5,000		10,000	2,500
Scenic Design Assistant	7,145		1,429	1,429	1,429	1,429	1,429	1,429	1,429			10,003	2,858
Costume Design Assistant	7,145		1,429	1,429	1,429	1,429	1,429					7,145	0
Lighting Design Assistant	7,145		1,429	1,429	1,429	1,429	1,429					7,145	0
Sound Design Assistant	3,750		750	750	750	750	750					3,750	0
Assistant Director	7,000		650	650	650	650	650	650	650	650		5,200	(1,800)
Prop Shopper	10,000	13,850					6,925			6,925		27,700	17,700
Production Assistants	4,000	250	500	500	500	500	500	500	500	500	250	4,500	500
	315,130	176,350	42,327	11,187	35,687	6,187	32,907	2,579	2,579	27,870	250	337,923	22,793

	Budget	Spent to Date as of 10/11/15	1st reh 10/25/15	11/01/15	Load-in 11/08/15	11/15/15	1st Preview 11/22/15	11/29/15	12/06/15	ON 12/13/15	Still Expected	Total	Over/(Under)
REHEARSAL/PREVIEW SALARIES													
Principals (Reh)	45,524		10,116	10,116	10,116	10,116	5,060					45,524	0
Understudies	30,687				6,744	6,744	3,711					17,199	(13,488)
Stage Managers	27,453	2,468	4,409	4,409	4,409	4,409	4,409	2,940				27,453	0
Producers	22,750	3,500				3,500	1,750					8,750	(14,000)
General Manager	21,125	3,250	3,250	3,250	3,250	3,250	3,250	1,625				21,125	0
Company Manager	13,416	2,064	2,064	2,064	2,064	2,064	2,064	1,032				13,416	0
Press Agent	10,099		2,244	2,244	2,244	2,244	1,123					10,099	0
Wardrobe	10,865					5,431	5,434					10,865	0
Hair/Make-up	2,576					1,288	1,288					2,576	0
Crew	4,200					1,850	2,350					4,200	0
	188,695	11,282	22,083	22,083	28,827	40,896	30,439	5,597	0	0	0	161,207	(27,488)
REHEARSAL/PREVIEW EXPENSE													
Theatre Expenses	96,000				96,000							96,000	0
Halls (Audition/Rehearsal)	9,000	5,160				4,500						9,660	660
Stage Manager & Departmental	3,500	1,600	600	600	600	600	250	250				4,500	1,000
	108,500	6,760	600	600	96,600	5,100	250	250	0	0	0	110,160	1,660
ADVERTISING & PUBLICITY													
Print/Media	75,000	30,131	33,631	13,923	25,673	3,859						107,218	32,218
Outdoor	0	10,000	10,000	2,500	31,500	2,500						56,500	56,500
Direct Marketing	225,000	46,159	79,606	750	9,990							136,505	(88,495)
Production/Printing	25,000	67,272	6,139	5,232	5,232	5,232	5,232					94,339	69,339
Front of House	25,000	12,728			7,272							20,000	(5,000)
Miscellaneous	0	8,045	2,600	1,300	1,300	1,221	1,800					16,266	16,266
Radio/TV	100,000	2,500				6,250	10,000					18,750	(81,250)
Marketing Expenses	17,700	22,506	3,000	1,544	1,894	1,300	2,645					32,890	15,190
Website Services	25,000	12,500	2,200	2,000	700	2,700	800	700			2,000	23,600	(1,400)
Press Agent Expenses	42,332	5,657	6,467	8,158	2,925	725	3,025	10,845	1,250	3,425		42,477	145
Playbill	2,500			2,500								2,500	0
	537,532	217,498	143,643	37,907	86,486	23,787	23,502	11,545	1,250	3,425	2,000	551,044	13,512

	Budget	as of 10/11/15 Spent to Date	1st reh 10/25/15	11/01/15	Load-in 11/08/15	11/15/15	1st Preview 11/22/15	11/29/15	12/06/15	ON 12/13/15	Still Expected	Total	Total Over/(Under)
GENERAL & ADMINISTRATIVE													
Producers Office	11,375	3,500	1,750	1,750	1,750	1,750	875					11,375	0
General Manager Office	8,125	2,500	1,250	1,250	1,250	1,250	625					8,125	0
Legal	40,000	20,250	20,000									40,250	250
Accounting	8,500		8,500									8,500	0
Payroll Taxes	28,304	1,091	3,312	3,312	4,324	6,134	6,258					24,432	(3,872)
Insurance	45,000	34,330										34,330	(10,670)
Pension & Welfare	48,295	809	3,691	5,300	6,350	6,350	6,350	6,350	6,350	6,745		48,295	0
Vacation/Sick	6,220		872	872	1,276	1,276	791	176				5,262	(958)
Hauling/Shipping	30,000				12,500	12,500	5,000					30,000	0
Teamsters	5,000				5,000	5,000	2,000					12,000	7,000
Shop Prep	30,000		15,000	15,000								30,000	0
Take-in, Hang & Rehearse	275,000			275,000								275,000	0
League Dues	450						450					450	0
Phone, Fax, Copying, Messenger	5,000	7,701	450	450	450	450	450	300	300	300		10,851	5,851
Transportation	25,500	4,533	19,491									24,024	(1,476)
Housing (Diamond)	12,364	271	1,764	1,764			1,764	1,764	1,764	1,470		10,561	(1,803)
Housing (Leon)	15,978		2,663	2,663	2,663	2,663	2,663	2,663				15,978	0
Housing (3 stars)	35,951		4,000	4,000	4,000	4,000	2,000					18,000	(17,951)
Per Diem (Leon)	4,200	1,000	700	700	700	700	700	700	500			5,700	1,500
Per Diem (Diamond)	4,200	600	600				600	600	600	500		3,500	(700)
Car Service	3,000						3,000					3,000	0
Opening Night	40,000	14,400			2,000				25,775			42,175	2,175
Broker Fees	24,000											0	(24,000)
Miscellaneous	2,181	3,731	200	200	100	100	100	100	100	100	181	4,912	2,731
	708,643	94,716	84,244	312,261	42,363	42,174	33,626	12,653	35,389	9,115	181	666,721	(41,922)
TOTAL EST. PROD. EXPENSE	2,246,000	676,676	389,397	404,038	392,989	121,143	153,724	35,624	39,718	40,410	2,431	2,256,150	10,150

ADVANCES AND DEPOSITS	Budget	as of 10/11/15 Spent to Date	1st reh 10/25/15	11/01/15	Load-in 11/08/15	11/15/15	1st Preview 11/22/15	11/29/15	12/06/15	ON 12/13/15	Still Expected	Total	Over/(Under)
Author	40,000	2,500	37,500									40,000	0
Director	0											0	0
Scenic Designer	4,376											0	(4,376)
Costume Designer	1,345	673					336			336		1,345	0
Lighting Designer	3,284	800	800				800			800		3,200	(84)
Sound Designer	2,500	1,250					625			625		2,500	0
AEA	135,604	121,215										121,215	(14,389)
ATPAM	16,565											0	(16,565)
Theatre Deposit	0											0	0
Housing Deposits	24,000											0	(24,000)
IATSE Bond	2,500			2,500								2,500	0
	230,174	124,515	40,223	2,500	0	0	1,761	0	0	1,761	0	170,760	(59,414)
RESERVE	423,826										423,826	423,826	0
TOTAL CAPITALIZATION	2,900,000	801,190	429,619	406,538	392,989	121,143	155,485	35,624	39,718	42,171	426,257	2,850,736	(49,264)

	Spent to Date	10/25/15	11/01/15	11/08/15	11/15/15	11/22/15	11/29/15	12/06/15	12/13/15	Still Expected		UNDER budget

as of 2/15/15

SAMPLE SHOW – 10-Week Out Gross Projection Chart

Week Ending	10 weeks	9 weeks	8 weeks	7 weeks	6 weeks	5 weeks	4 weeks	3 weeks	2 weeks	1 week	Net Gross	Week of Growth	Comments
11/23/14							$43,175	$56,493	$89,488	$110,734	$189,185	$78,452	5 perfs only
11/30/14						$29,302	$46,095	$70,113	$89,366	$142,799	$246,719	$103,920	Thanksgiving
12/07/14					$78,569	$96,802	$112,229	$123,122	$157,848	$184,040	$271,581	$87,541	
12/14/14				$41,964	$59,074	$73,544	$88,251	$109,488	$132,767	$172,818	$240,016	$67,198	
12/21/14			$22,231	$34,399	$49,713	$70,025	$81,977	$104,351	$134,051	$176,099	$238,736	$62,637	
12/28/14		$7,965	$13,853	$18,861	$23,171	$32,969	$40,017	$55,548	$83,515	$138,839	$197,634	$58,795	Christmas
01/04/15	$7,288	$8,922	$11,249	$17,361	$24,825	$29,199	$42,766	$66,887	$123,201	$210,521	$343,215	$132,694	New Year's (9)
01/11/15	$7,153	$11,187	$15,767	$20,653	$25,380	$34,242	$51,734	$74,735	$109,788	$142,042	$229,470	$87,428	7 shows
01/18/15	$11,486	$15,976	$18,622	$23,581	$31,438	$47,197	$64,088	$87,797	$110,312	$158,061	$277,261	$119,200	MLK w/e
01/25/15	$3,429	$5,719	$8,330	$11,398	$20,449	$30,662	$44,404	$60,339	$99,634	$170,106	$239,740	$69,634	
02/01/15	$2,918	$6,974	$9,331	$11,745	$20,035	$30,301	$37,149	$66,533	$119,412	$181,758	$266,314	$84,556	
02/08/15	$193	$684	$1,007	$1,100	$3,921	$6,855	$17,020	$44,079	$93,134	$138,610	$216,013	$77,404	
02/15/15	$686	$819	$1,005	$3,108	$3,919	$12,561	$27,195	$46,574	$67,993	$101,771			President's Day
02/22/15	$949	$1,297	$5,103	$12,131	$18,269	$43,382	$62,667	$81,456	$115,050				
03/01/15	$891	$1,234	$3,286	$11,404	$25,235	$39,810	$59,470	$91,745					
03/08/15	$1,212	$1,910	$21,258	$26,883	$29,037	$32,588	$43,731						
03/15/15	$741	$1,564	$1,793	$4,031	$10,007	$13,694							
03/22/15	$2,848	$3,020	$8,075	$7,625	$15,438								
03/29/15	$935	$1,387	$2,527	$4,816									
04/05/15	$5,438	$7,850	$12,618										
04/12/15	$4,468	$8,862											
04/19/15	$2,441												
Average per column	$3,317	$5,335	$9,753	$15,691	$27,405	$38,946	$53,873	$75,951	$108,968	$156,015	$246,324	$85,788	

ADVERTISING COST EFFECTIVENESS TRACKING
DIRECT RESPONSE

NAME	ON SALE/ DROPS	PERF DATES	PRICES	COST	PRICE KEY	CODE	TO DATE	PROFIT/(LOSS)
Playbill Blast	9/19 – 4/8	11/18-4/8	84/63/44.45/68.95 91/63/44.5/69	15,000.00	B	SFPBX909	108,389.40	93,389.40
Broadway Box # 1	10/5-4/8	11/18-4/8	84/63/44.45/68.95 91/63/44.5/69	7,000.00	B	SFBX916	149,928.30	142,928.30
Broadway Box #2	12/9-4/8	12/13-4/8	84/63/44.45/68.95 91/63/44.5/69	7,600.00	BA	SFBX129	131,829.40	124,229.40
Broadway Box #3	1/17/2012	1/17 - 3/04	84/63/44.45/68.95 91/63/44.5/69	7,600.00	B	SFBBX14	33,165.75	25,565.75
Broadway Box #4	2/10/2012	2/10-2/26	84/63/44.45/68.95 91/63/44.5/69	7,600.00	B	SFBBX211	74,458.40	66,858.40
Telecharge #1	10/18-4/8	11/18-4/8	84/63/69/44.5/33.5 91/63/69/44.5/33.5	14,825.00	B	SFTCX926 SFTCX14	69,823.85 273.00	55,271.85
Telecharge #2	1/10/2012	1/10 - 03/04	84/63/69/44.5/33.5 91/63/69/44.5/33.5	300.00	B BB	SFTCX14 SFTC4PAK	36,246.90 8,593.20	44,540.10
TheatreMania	11/18-4/8	11/18-4/8	84/63/69/44.5/33.5 91/63/69/44.5/33.5	6,650.00	B	SFTM926	98,135.75	91,485.75
Plum Benefits	9/21-4/8	11/18-4/8	84/63/69/44.5/33.5 91/63/69/44.5/33.5	29,580.78	B	SFPLM920	220,107.80	190,527.02
Friends & Family	9/21-4/8	11/18-4/8	84/63/69/44.5/33.5 91/63/69/44.5/33.5	-	B	SFFNF927	61,592.35	61,592.35
Direct Mail	10/21-4/8	11/18-4/8	84/63/69/44.5/33.5 91/63/69/44.5/33.5	96,000.00	B & Y	SFDM927	275,015.10	179,015.10

NY Tix	12/6-4/8	12/6-4/8	84/63/69/44.5/33.5 91/63/69/44.5/33.5	2,352.94	B	SFTIX1027	16,787.35	14,434.41
Broadway Fan Club	11/15-4/8	11/18-4/8	84/63/69/44.5/33.5 91/63/69/44.5/33.5		B	SFBFC1115	6,826.55	6,826.55
NYC Pocket Guide	11/15-4/8	11/18-4/8	84/63/69/44.5/33.5 91/63/69/44.5/33.5		B	SFNYC113	4,133.95	4,133.95
Broadway Week	12/15/2011	11/18-4/8	96/68/74/49.5/33.5	2000.00	N	BW2012	304,593.50	302,593.50

14

Prime, Decline, Death, and Afterlife: The Four Ages of Theater

All the world's a stage,
And all the men and women merely players;
They have their exits and their entrances;
And one man in his time plays many parts,
His acts being seven ages. At first the infant,
Mewling and puking in the nurse's arms;
And then the whining school-boy, with his satchel
And shining morning face, creeping like snail
Unwillingly to school. And then the lover,
Sighing like furnace, with a woeful ballad
Made to his mistress' eyebrow. Then a soldier,
Full of strange oaths, and bearded like the pard,
Jealous in honour, sudden and quick in quarrel,
Seeking the bubble reputation
Even in the cannon's mouth. And then the justice,
In fair round belly with good capon lin'd,

With eyes severe and beard of formal cut,
Full of wise saws and modern instances;
And so he plays his part. The sixth age shifts
Into the lean and slipper'd pantaloon,
With spectacles on nose and pouch on side;
His youthful hose, well sav'd, a world too wide
For his shrunk shank; and his big manly voice,
Turning again toward childish treble, pipes
And whistles in his sound. Last scene of all,
That ends this strange eventful history,
Is second childishness and mere oblivion;
Sans teeth, sans eyes, sans taste, sans everything.
—*As You Like It*, Act II, scene 7

Just as Shakespeare, in Jacques's famous speech from *As You Like It*, describes the seven ages of man, so too a play goes through different stages in its life. Previous chapters have already discussed the earliest phases: pre-production, rehearsal, the tech period, previews, and opening. This chapter will provide an overview of the issues related to maintaining a healthy show, grappling with a declining show, closing a show, and tending to the ongoing affairs of a show in its life after Broadway.

PRIME: WEEKLY MAINTENANCE

Every show, as long as it is running, has standard operating procedures that must be executed every week. One of these is payroll, which has to be calculated, called in, received, checked, and distributed—some checks are handed out at the theater on Thursday, the weekly pay day, while others must be mailed. In addition, a variety of paperwork—wage statements mandated by the NYS Wage Theft Protection Act, royalty cover sheets, union benefit reports, box office statements, weekly profit and loss accounting statements—accompanies many of these checks and has to be prepared, printed, and stuffed in the appropriate payroll envelopes along with the payment. Payroll is the responsibility of the company manager and is normally checked and signed by the GM.

Bills must be paid. The GM will authorize which bills should be paid, but the company manager will review the invoices, code the expenses according to a set list of accounting codes, and cut the checks preparatory to handing them to the GM for signature.

All the collective bargaining entities (I am avoiding the word union, as some are technically societies or guilds) that the producer deals with— Equity, ATPAM, the **Dramatists Guild of America (DGA)**, SDC, USA, Local 764, Local 798, IATSE—require weekly contributions to various benefit funds. These include dues, pension, health, and annuity, and all checks must be accompanied by a report that breaks down the lump payment to the fund into its various member constituents, listing each person's name, social security number, and the exact amount of his or her individual contribution.

Royalties must be calculated for each person receiving either a fixed or percentage royalty. The check must be accompanied by a cover sheet and, if applicable, a copy of the box office statement (usually just the one for the last performance of the week, which states the final gross on which royalties will be calculated) and profit and loss statement for that week. In addition, a copy of the check and all accompanying paperwork must go to the governing union, guild, or society as well.

Weekly profit and loss (P&L) statements are initially prepared by the company manager and show accountant, or bookkeeper, then carefully reviewed by the general manager. While always following correct and strict accounting guidelines, there sometimes is room for discretion on how accruals and amortizations are accounted for. This, in turn, can adjust the bottom line profit or loss figure for a given week. If individuals are currently being paid on the basis of net profits, this change will affect their royalty calculations.

Usually on Tuesday night, the company manager receives the previous week's theater settlement and settlement check at the theater. The settlement is the document that states the final gross for the week due to the company and then details all of the theater's expenses that are withheld from it—theater salaries plus benefits and payroll taxes (for the treasurers, house manager, ushers, porters, stage doormen, stagehands, musicians, if applicable), house expenses, and the theater's royalty—thereby reducing that gross to a net figure. All of this information must be backed up by copies of payroll and bills and needs to be carefully reviewed by the CM. A check to the show for the resultant net figure is attached to the settlement.

It should go without saying by now that in any week in which the show is playing, in any age of its life, the general manager, often with the assistance of the company manager, will be expected to compile figures, send out reports, and offer forecasts of the show's finances.

PRIME: LONG-TERM MAINTENANCE

If a show is fortunate enough to continue running, a variety of concerns will need to be addressed for the long-term maintenance of a show.

Weekly P&Ls are an initial draft of the show's accounting. They are typically collected into a report that covers a four-week cycle of performances, which is then reviewed by the show accountant, GM, and lead producer(s). Once all three parties have signed off on it, the report is printed by the accountant's office, delivered to the GM's office, and, from there, mailed to all the investors and producers, accompanied by a cover note from either the producer or GM.

If a show runs, the assumption is that it will begin to accumulate weekly operating profits. As this occurs, the GM will recommend to the producer that the show should issue a profit distribution—initially as a return of capital just to the investors, until the amount returned equals the show's production costs. Subsequent distributions will be of net profits and will go to the investors, producers, and any other individual or entity that has been awarded a percentage of net profits. Profit distributions are often done on a separate payroll account run by the payroll service, so that the service can keep track of, and ultimately issue an end-of-year tax document to, each investor. The calculation of who gets how much of the amount being distributed is typically done by the GM. God bless Excel.

Over time, it is conceivable that members of the cast (not on term contracts) and crew may give notice, may need to be terminated (always for "just cause," as their union requires), or will reach the end of their term of employment. This will necessitate the GM negotiating new contracts and hiring replacements for them.

In a long run, it is conceivable costumes may wear out or future cast replacements will be of a different size. In either event, new costumes may eventually be needed, and if this is anticipated, the GM should have a clear idea of the costs involved and should instruct the accountant to establish a weekly accrual for such an eventuality.

The logo, or principal advertising image of a show (think the Phantom's mask in *The Phantom of the Opera* or the waif-like Cossette in *Les Miserables*), often requires tweaking over the life of a show to keep it fresh in the public's mind and to appeal to changing markets. Imagine a pebble being thrown into a pond and creating ever-widening ripples. The first demographic a show usually tries to reach in its advertising is the dedicated, New York–based theatergoer. Over time, the reach should extend to the tri-state suburbs, referred to as the bridge-and-tunnel crowd. If the show becomes well established, one has to eventually reach domestic tourists coming to New York for a visit. Finally, and most likely only needed for a long-run musical, you want to make sure that international tourists have your show on their radar.

Periodically, the accountant will do bank reconciliations, which will include a list of checks that have not cleared. The GM should review the list and note which checks are several months old. It is likely the parties to whom these checks were issued will have to be contacted, their current addresses confirmed, and the checks cancelled and reissued. If a payroll check is involved (remember the Amelia story!), the payroll company will have to be informed of any stop payments and reissues.

DECLINE

Over time, a show will exhaust its market and business will begin to fade. Grosses will drop, and the show will hover close to its breakeven point. In this instance, there are a number of things a GM should set in motion.

Cuts

When losses are looming, try to reduce costs by cutting expenses wherever possible. Theater owners can be generous in reducing the profit portion of their expense package, particularly the guaranteed rent component. It is in a theater owner's best interest to keep his or her theater lit (open): the theater passes on most of its operating expenses to the show, and a dark (unoccupied) theater is expensive to carry. A reduction in expenses is most likely to be agreed to if there is not another production hovering, waiting to move into the theater the moment your show closes. Sometimes a rent reduction, or cut, is agreed to for a limited period of time, perhaps four weeks, to buy the show time to see if it can turn its fortunes around.

Advertising and marketing is another area in which one can look for cuts, but of course this can also be self-defeating, as both provide the principal means of selling tickets. Still, an upcoming, expensive endeavor, such as a direct mail piece, can be rethought and possibly replaced with a less expensive measure, such as an email blast, if it is not yet past the endeavor's cancellation deadline.

The equipment shops—scenic, lighting, and sound—can also be generous in reducing their costs to help the show stay alive. Even a 25 percent reduction in the weekly rental can be a help.

Three expenses the producer has total control over are his weekly office fee, his weekly producer fee (if any), and his weekly royalty. Any and all of these can be cut if the producer agrees and can afford to subsist without them.

If one is paying a star significantly over minimum, one always has the option of asking his or her agent to agree to a reduction in the star's base salary. If agreed to, a rider would have to be filed with Equity stating the new amount. Of course, there is no guarantee the star will agree, but as we say in the business, "You don't ask, you don't get." It is also helpful, in this instance, for the producer to be able to say that he has cut some of the payments to himself, as outlined in the preceding paragraph.

Finally, as discussed in a previous chapter, now may be the time to switch the calculation of royalties from a gross to a net basis. However, if the show is expected to have primarily losing weeks, breakeven weeks, or even just Grey Zone weeks, and an individual's minimum weekly guarantee is the same in both scenarios, this switch may not make much difference. One would have to calculate the royalty figures in both instances to be confident that making this change was worthwhile, as well as feel confident that the show really was on its deathbed and, unlike Rasputin, was not going to pop up again unexpectedly!

WAIVERS

All royalty recipients with the exception of the producer are under the jurisdiction of a collective bargaining agreement, which will contain provisions for protecting its member's royalties from a unilateral (on the part of the producer!) and arbitrary reduction. That said, most of these same collective bargaining agents also acknowledge how hard many shows struggle to stay alive and will provide language that allows a producer, under certain conditions and for limited periods of time, to waive and/or defer its members' royalties in order to lower running costs. As an example, United Scenic Artists allows a producer to waive the designers' royalties below their specified minimums for up to eight weeks, which need not be consecutive, in losing weeks only. If the waiver weeks are consecutive, then the allowable period may not exceed four weeks. If so elected, the designer must be notified in writing, with a copy to USA. SDC has abrogated its right of consent to a reduction of its members' royalties as long as the applicable minimums are paid but also provides language for waivers below these minimums, for a maximum of four weeks, as long as an agreement is signed by both the member and the producer and is filed with the society.

DEFERRALS

Deferrals provide a mechanism for not paying someone now but offer the possibility, not the guarantee, of repaying the deferred amount at a later date if finances improve. The deferred payments are noted and kept track of and have a negotiated trigger for repayment—say, if the gross exceeds some figure beyond the show's new, reduced breakeven point, plus a 20 percent margin as a cushion. One would have to look at the collective amount of the deferrals and crunch the numbers before confidently identifying the trigger for repayment.

DEATH (CLOSING)

Despite the bravura tagline of the original *Cats* ("Now and Forever!") every show does eventually close. (Not that it can't subsequently be revived!)

When one sees the writing on the wall, usually by tracking the advance breakdown of future weeks ("We fall off the cliff right after New Year's!"), the ideal is to plan an announced closing date at least several weeks in advance. This allows the show to orchestrate an advertising campaign, often in the form of a countdown ("only three weeks left . . ." "final eight performances," "last chance to see . . .") to try to grab the attention, and the business, of every last ticket buyer who has kept meaning to see the show but just hasn't gotten around to it yet. Of course, not every show will have this luxury. Sometimes, especially when a show opens to universally scathing reviews, has been plagued with technical problems and nasty in-fighting, is way over budget, has little or no reserve left, and/or the star has started drinking, the producers, demoralized by the challenges of making Art and faced with the prospect of losing their homes, will just decide to close the show without putting up a fight. I have worked on at least two shows that wound up closing precipitously the same week that they opened. It is a heartbreaking, devastating experience to witness and man-age, as people's hopes, dreams, investment, and employment are suddenly snatched from them. While a GM personally has no liability for a show's losses, he or she is naturally selected to embody responsibility and can feel a production's failure deeply. All that said, sometimes closing swiftly, especially if the show has no advance sales or reserve left, is the only sane, responsible thing to do.

One should also be mindful if the show has offered any trade tickets (complimentary tickets given as barter, i.e., in lieu of cash, for things like extra radio spots that are added onto a cash buy) for future performances one now no longer expects to play. Unless you can convert those tickets to earlier performances, or convince a colleague who has a show in previews to take them over, the show could be charged the cash value of any unful-filled ticket trade.

Once the decision to close has been made, the first thing that needs to be done is to generate the appropriate notices that are contractually required. Usually, the first one goes to the theater owner. Next, the com-pany, cast and crew, must be informed. A company notice, copy going to all the appropriate unions, must be posted at the theater no later than half hour prior to the curtain of the first performance in a week, stating that the show will close after the final performance that week. If this does not happen until later in the week, the producer is liable for paying one eighth of weekly salaries for each performance less than eight for which notice was given. Often, as a courtesy and to help soften the blow of imminent unemployment, the PSM will be asked to call a company meeting shortly before half hour, so that the producer and general manager can go over to the theater, personally inform the company that the notice is going up, and answer any questions. The purpose of this meeting is rarely a surprise to anyone—who knows better than the people in the theater that they have been playing to half-full houses—but it is inevitably a sad occasion.

I recall one actress breaking down and sobbing after the announcement was made.

Any Equity member signed to a term contract must also receive his or her own individual closing notice (with a copy to Equity). If the show has any stars, it is considered proper form to call them or their agents and personally inform them of the decision to close. The production stage manager should also be called, as should the technical supervisor, who needs to begin planning the load-out of the physical production.

Finally, the equipment rental shops, royalty recipients, all the various unions, and their union benefit funds all need to be informed of the show's closing date. Otherwise, they will keep sending you invoices or notices that you are delinquent for payments due for weeks you didn't play!

Once benefit payments for the final playing week's salaries have been issued, plus, in the case of Equity, payment for any vacation or sick pay that is due, the unions should immediately be requested to begin the process of releasing the show's bond. (Go back and look at the bonds in the production budget example—in this instance, Actors' Equity is holding a little over $197,000 of the show's money!). Equity often has the most members employed of any theatrical union and, therefore, the biggest bond. They insist on a six-week review period prior to releasing a bond, as they have to receive assurance from each of their internal departments—dues, pension, welfare, annuity—that all the show's obligations have been met and no payment to any individual is unaccounted for in a single playing week of the run.

After notices have been issued, the PSM needs to schedule a load-out production meeting in the theater. The technical supervisor will lead it, and the producer, GM, CM, and all stagehand department heads—carpentry, electrics, props, wardrobe, hair—should be present. Everyone's packing needs and trucking should be reviewed, department by department. If costumes are to be saved, how does wardrobe plan to get the clothes to the drycleaners and back in time to be packed and loaded out? Who needs packing materials? Are any props or costumes rented and need to be returned? Does the wardrobe supervisor or the PSM have a work box or desk that needs to be delivered somewhere for storage? The tech supervisor will have to schedule the crew calls, find the manpower for them, and arrange for trucking as well as trucking permits. Also, it is important to decide if the physical elements are to be stored for possible future usage or tossed in a dumpster and carted away. Load-outs are not only complex, they are also expensive.

NOTE: Several years ago, a $12,000,000 musical called *Dance of the Vampires* closed abruptly after opening. It was a big show, and I remember hearing through the grapevine that the expected load-out costs were rumored to be in the vicinity of $1,000,000. For the first time in my experience, the show, to help raise money, offered various items, mostly props, for sale on Ebay. Such unique memorabilia as a string of plastic sausages was now available to the highest bidder.

Contrary to this very public appeal, shows will sometimes auction off props or costumes to company members. I myself admit to purchasing a number of items for my home that came from theatrical sets, including what I fondly refer to as the Rose Kennedy drapes. Only if questioned will I admit that they actually belonged to the *set* of a play about Rose Kennedy, not to Rose herself.

Once the closing date is set, the insurance broker should be contacted to terminate the existing insurance policies. In the case of the workers' comp policy, if the premium was based on annual salaries and the show's run was shorter than that, an audit needs to be scheduled that may result in the show receiving a partial return of the premium. And if it was decided to store any element of the physical production, a new storage policy must be put into place. Storage, though an ongoing expense, makes sense if one believes there may be a national tour that could use the existing elements, or if there may be regional or stock productions that might be interested in buying or renting any of the production elements.

NOTE: Many years ago, I worked on the award-winning original New York production of Sam Shepard's *A Lie of the Mind*. In one scene, the action called for a hunter to enter onstage with the hind end of a mule deer slung over his shoulder. This was a difficult, and expensive, prop to come up with; it had to be specially built, and to give the appearance of reality, it was covered in actual deerskin. When the production closed, it was put into storage.

A few years later, the Royal Court Theatre in London wanted to do the play and was interested in renting our mule deer prop for their production, mule deer not being native to England. I was still an office assistant at the time, and it devolved to me to arrange for the transportation of this exotic item. Problem was, every time I called an airline and said, "Hi, I'd like to arrange for the transportation of the rear end of a mule deer," they hung up on me!

Depending on whether or not any cast members were brought in from out of town, and what kind of housing was arranged for them, return flights may have to be arranged, and notice of termination of a rental agreement may need to be given.

AFTERLIFE

So, now the show has closed, the physical production has loaded out, the final payroll has been run, and the company manager has left, hopefully for a brief vacation before starting on a new project. Now what?

Unless the show has been a big flop and has come and gone so quickly that it is unlikely there will be any interest in future productions, there will be periodic maintenance for the GM to tend to. The annual fee outlined in the GM's agreement is intended to provide compensation for these duties. They will include such things as:

- Paying the monthly storage bill, if taken.
- Reviewing the paperwork and depositing the checks for any stock and amateur licensing income, if applicable. The licensing agents tend to mail out statements and checks to the author's agent twice a year. The author's agent then cuts a check to the original production for its share of this subsidiary income and mails it to the GM's

office. If the author received an advance, the advance will have to be worked off before any additional income is received, and the semiannual reports will have to be carefully tracked to follow this progress.

- If subsidiary income is received, then occasional profit distributions will have to be executed.

- Bank reconciliations will continue to be necessary, and uncleared checks for any significant period of time will need to be followed up on, cancelled, and reissued.

- Occasionally, an investor will inform you that he has changed his address or even his legal name. This will necessitate the GM modifying mailing labels and mail merge files in his office, as well as informing the payroll service, accountant, and production attorney, as applicable, of the change.

- As long as the producing entity is not officially dissolved and remains in business, the accountant will prepare annual year-end accounting statements, which must first be reviewed and approved and then mailed out by the GM.

- There will also be year-end tax reporting—W-2s, 1099s and K-1 forms—that have to be checked by the accountant and mailed out by the GM.

- And, of course, if the show was successful enough to spawn a national touring production, licensed regional productions, and/or foreign productions, the GM will probably be hired to manage it, in the first case, or to be available to advise and coordinate matters, in the second or third cases.

BEYOND PAPERWORK

Up to this point, this book has primarily concentrated on the tangible, practical, largely administrative aspects of a general manager's job. But there is another side to the job as well, and to not mention it would be a disservice to the position.

A GM serves as a kind of figurehead, or leader, representing both the producer as well as the production on many different levels. A GM should always strive to be positive, fair minded, efficient, and helpful. A GM sets the tone of the working environment that is the show experience, both personally in his or her own office and, by proxy, through the demeanor of the company manager who is the producer and GM's daily representative at the theater.

A GM may be able to contribute a solution if something is not working with the show, particularly in the technical or preview period. Of course, it is vital that any creative suggestions are offered at the appropriate time and to the appropriate person—that is, to the producer in private, never directly to the director or author.

NOTE: I have an esteemed colleague who once watched, during tech, as the director of a show became more and more frustrated with the crafting of a critical scene change. The lighting designer and stage manager kept cueing the scene in different ways, but it was not what the director wanted and the communication had broken down. As general manager, my colleague went to the producer and explained what she thought the director wanted—to convey a sense of memory, regret, and aching loss. The producer took my colleague to the director, who agreed with her, and she sat down to explain the cueing in terms of the musical interlude and its emotional impact on the cue. It took someone with an outside eye to come in and clarify the communication, through the proper channels. Sometimes it is the GM's job to be that eye.

Finally, a GM plays a very important psychological role—his or her relationship to the producer is an intense one, full of confidences and trust (I once had a producer actually say to me "You've got to save me from myself!"). At various times, a GM serves as an advisor, a confidante, a therapist, a father confessor, a support, a protector, a cohort, a fixer, and a bad cop to the producer's good cop. The two parties typically speak on the phone and/or email each other many, many times a day, every day. Most producers feel they need access to their GM whenever anything important or urgent occurs, no matter how early or late the hour, or whether it is a weekend or a national holiday. You are on call twenty-four/seven.

NOTE: In the musical *On the Twentieth Century* (music by Cy Coleman, book and lyrics by Betty Comden and Adolf Green), the characters of Owen and Oliver succinctly describe the downside of working for their colorful but flop-prone producer, Oscar Jaffe: "Working for Jaffe, though continually bracing, also destroys the heart and liver!"

Working in the commercial theater entails grappling with an enormous number of exciting, challenging, and complex details. Not to mention individuals like the fictitious Oscar Jaffe, mentioned above! All these concerns and personalities need to be general managed by an experienced professional. No book, not even this one, can do this for you. I hope, by now, you are no longer mystified by what a general manager does and can appreciate just how invaluable a good GM is for guiding and protecting both a producer and the multimillion dollar venture that is a Broadway show today.

Glossary

"10 out of 12s": The final week in a show's technical and rehearsal period immediately prior to the first paid public performance, during which certain unions allow their members to work for ten consecutive hours, as long as they have two, one-hour breaks during their call.

Actors' Equity Association (AEA, or Equity): The actor's and stage manager's union.

additional weekly compensation (AWC): A fixed weekly royalty often negotiated for designers.

approved production contract (APC): The contract between the Dramatists Guild, representing authors, and Broadway producers. The APC has two versions, one for plays and the other for musicals.

assistant director (AD): An assistant to the director who works closely with the director and takes notes from the first day of rehearsal, if not one week prior to that date, through all rehearsals, tech, and previews, up to opening night.

assistant stage manager (ASM): An assistant to the production stage manager who is required by AEA to be hired one week prior to the start of rehearsals.

Association of Theatrical Press Agents and Managers (ATPAM): The union representing press agents, company managers, and house managers.

breakeven (nut): The box office gross at which the show's revenue exactly covers its running costs, resulting in zero profit or loss for the week.

The Broadway League: The trade organization representing Broadway producers, theater owners, general managers, and nationwide "road" presenters. Aside from providing invaluable educational, audience development, and industry-promoting functions, the League, as it is commonly referred to, also negotiates all the collective bargaining labor agreements with the various unions, guilds, and societies that comprise the theatrical industry on its members' behalf.

capacity gross: The maximum amount of ticket sales one can hope for, based on 100 percent of the theater's seating capacity being sold, all at full price (no discounts, unsold, or complimentary tickets included). This calculation is often made without taking into account any premium priced ticket sales, so a show selling a large amount of premium seats may report a gross that is qualified as exceeding 100 percent of its capacity gross.

capitalization: The total amount of investment stated in the show's operating agreement that the producer needs to raise in order to form the entity that will finance the production. Often a range of capital, comprising a minimum original capital amount and a maximum original capital amount, is indicated. It is possible to form the entity by achieving the lower threshold, but it is wise to aim for raising the higher amount.

company manager (CM): The person who is heavily involved in the day-to-day administration of the company, such as reading all the contracts; setting up, calculating, and calling in the weekly payroll; paying bills as directed; overseeing house seat requests; making sure that union benefits are paid and sent to the appropriate fund office, enclosing with them explicit cover sheets detailing what contribution should be credited to which individual's account; keeping track of ticket sales and advising which performances or price sections are weak and need attention; reviewing the weekly theater settlement that accompanies the show's settlement check, checking all the back-up as well as the arithmetic; sending out royalty statements along with cover sheets and accounting statements; and submitting new pricing information, performance schedule changes, or discount code requests to the box office, among other things.

Dramatists Guild of America (DGA): The collective bargaining entity for authors.

favored nations: A term used in contract negotiation and appearing in contracts that stipulates that everyone on the same level or tier—all stars billed above the title, for example—will receive the same terms and conditions, that is, no one else on that same level is getting a better deal.

fixed weekly expenses: Weekly operating costs that do not fluctuate from week to week, but remain constant.

general manager (GM): The chief business advisor to a producer; the person who prepares budgets, negotiates contracts, and maintains financial overview of a production.

Grey Zone: A range of box office gross, between the show's breakeven figure and 110 percent of that figure, in which the producer is granted relief from paying full royalties, which would cause the week to show a loss. Instead, the producer is able to pay percentage royalty recipients a prenegotiated minimum weekly guarantee, plus some percentage of operating profits, if any.

gross gross: The full box office gross, before any allowable deductions are made (for union pension payments, group sales and credit card commissions, ticket printing fees, etc.) to arrive at an adjusted net gross, on which royalties are calculated.

GWBOR: Acronym for gross weekly box office receipts.

house seats: Choice location seats specifically reserved for a top creative's personal use and therefore not part of the inventory that is on sale to the general public. House seats are not complimentary: they have to be purchased.

International Alliance of Theatrical Stage Employees (IATSE): The national stagehand's union.

letter of agreement (LOA): A nonunion employment contract in the form of a letter.

Local 764: The New York City local for union wardrobe supervisors, assistants, and dressers.

Local 798: The New York City local for union hair and make-up supervisors and their assistants.

Media Payment: An additional payment required by Actors' Equity Association, typically 2 percent of the current actor minimum. This payment allows producers the right to record the show, in whole or in part, and use this footage in a wide variety of noncommercial, advertising, and marketing purposes to promote the show, where no income is earned for its use. Outlets for this footage include the show's own website, talk shows where members of the cast appear, or television news programs that do a feature on the show or review the show.

mice type: Extremely small type, usually at the end of a discount offer, that contains a variety of disclaimers, such as "subject to availability".

minimum weekly guarantee (MWG): What the creative team (author, director, producer, licensor) receives in losing weeks, breakeven weeks, or weeks where the gross does not exceed 110 percent of breakeven.

net gross: The industry-approved adjusted gross gross, after very specific, allowable costs that the company does not receive have been deducted from it. These deductions include things like union pension payments, group sales and credit card commissions, ticket printing fees, etc. It is this net gross figure on which royalties are calculated.

operating budget: A budget detailing the show's estimated weekly operating expenses. It will include unvarying fixed weekly expenses and additional variable expenses (those dependent on the fluctuating box office gross), will identify the show's weekly breakeven, will show what the maximum capacity gross is (100 percent of full-price ticket sales) and what percentage of capacity gross the show's breakeven represents, and will give several different recoupment scenarios showing how many weeks it would take to recoup the show's production costs at different percentages of gross capacity.

option agreement: A document that grants the producer the exclusive right to produce an identified dramatic property in a specific area within a limited period of time for a particular sum of money.

paper: Complimentary tickets.

Pinks: IATSE crew members who are solely dedicated to operating and maintaining the show's technical needs, in contrast to Local 1 stagehands who work for the theater. The nickname is in reference to the color of their contracts.

premium seats: Choice orchestra seats that, due to their location, are sold at a premium—that is, at a higher price than the regular top orchestra seating price.

preview: Paid public performances prior to the show's official opening night.

production assistant (PA): A runner who may be needed in the general manager's office as well as in the rehearsal room to assist the stage managers.

production budget: A budget that tells the producer how much money will need to be raised to produce the show and get it to the first paid public performance. This budget has three major components: production costs, advances/deposits/bonds, and a reserve.

production costs: The major part of a production budget; those expenses spent to mount the show and get it to its first paid public performance or preview. Thereafter, expenses are classified as operating expenses.

production stage manager (PSM): The head stage manager on a production.

recoupment scenario: A calculation showing how many weeks it would take a show to recoup its production costs at a specific box office gross, which represents a certain percentage of capacity, such as, sixteen weeks at 70 percent of capacity, twelve weeks at 80 percent of capacity, etc.

return on investment (ROI): A measure of how well something that cost money performed.

Securities and Exchange Commission (SEC): The federal agency whose primary responsibilities include enforcing federal securities laws and regulating the securities industry.

Stage Directors and Choreographers Society (SDC): The collective bargaining agent for directors and choreographers.

term increment: An additional weekly payment required by AEA when one wants to contract and hold an actor for a set amount of time, say six months. This payment precludes the actor from exercising his or her normal right to give two-week notice and leave the show before the end of his or her term. Of course, the producer still has the right to close the show by giving one week's company closing notice.

Theatre Development Fund (TDF): A not-for-profit organization for the performing arts whose mission is to make theatre affordable and accessible to all. One of their programs involves soliciting likely-to-remain unsold seats from shows and selling them in advance, at a significant discount, to their members.

TKTS: Another program belonging to TDF, in which TDF–operated ticket booths offer anyone willing to stand in line the opportunity to purchase same-day discounted theater tickets, likely to otherwise go unsold.

United Scenic Artists (USA): The collective bargaining agent for all the theatrical designers—scenic, costume, lighting, and sound.

variable expenses: Those weekly expenses that fluctuate from week to week, depending on the amount of the box office gross.

vesting: A threshold number of performances that, if met, qualifies the producer to elect a series of subsequent production rights if he or she so chooses, as well as to participate in a share of the author's subsidiary income from sources of exploitation that were originally reserved by the author.

wrap: The total amount of ticket sales sold on a given day, starting at one minute after midnight and ending at midnight the same day, from all sales sources (box office window, telephones, Internet, remote outlets).

Index

BOOKS FROM ALLWORTH PRESS

Acting in LA
by Kristina Sexton (5½ x 8¼, 208 pages, paperback, $19.99)

The Actor Uncovered
by Michael Howard (6 x 9, 240 pages, hardcover, $24.99)

Building the Successful Theater Company
by Lisa Mulcahy (6 x 9, 284 pages, paperback, $24.99)

Business and Legal Forms for Theater (Second Edition)
by Charles Grippo (8½ x 11, 192 pages, paperback, $24.99)

The Business of Broadway
by Mitch Weiss and Perri Gaffney (6 x 9, 292 pages, hardcover, $24.99)

The Business of Theatrical Design
by James Moody (6 x 9, 304 pages, paperback, $19.95)

Fundamentals of Theatrical Design
by Karen Brewster and Melissa Shafer (6 x 9, 256 pages, paperback, $27.50)

Great Producers
by Iris Dorbian (6 x 9, 208 pages, paperback, $24.95)

Leadership in the Performing Arts
by Tobie S. Stein (5½ x 8¼, 252 pages, paperback, $19.99)

Making It on Broadway
by David Wienir and Jodie Langel with Jason Alexander (6 x 9, 288 pages, paperback, $19.95)

Movement for Actors
by Nicole Potter, Barbara Adrian, and Mary Fleischer (6 x 9, 376 pages, paperback, $22.99)

The Perfect Stage Crew
by John Kaluta (6 x 9, 272 pages, paperback, $19.99)

Performing Arts Management
by Tobie S. Stein and Jessica Bathurst (8½ x 11, 552 pages, paperback, $50.00)

Running Theaters
by Duncan Webb (6 9, 256 pages, paperback, $19.95)